21st Century bars

21st Century bars

Edited by Andrew Hall

images
Publishing

Published in Australia in 2010 by
The Images Publishing Group Pty Ltd
ABN 89 059 734 431
6 Bastow Place, Mulgrave, Victoria 3170, Australia
Tel: +61 3 9561 5544 Fax: +61 3 9561 4860
books@imagespublishing.com
www.imagespublishing.com

National Library of Australia Cataloguing-in-Publication entry:

Title:	21st century bars.
Edition:	1st ed.
ISBN:	9781864703740 (hbk.)
Subjects:	Bars (Drinking Establishments)—Pictorial Works.
	Bars (Drinking Establishments)—Designs and Plans.
Dewey Number: 647.95	

Edited by Andrew Hall

Designed by The Graphic Image Studio Pty Ltd, Mulgrave, Australia
www.tgis.com.au

Pre-publishing services by Mission Productions Limited, Hong Kong
Printed on 140 gsm Chinese matt art paper by Paramount Printing
Company Limited Hong Kong

IMAGES has included on its website a page for special notices in relation to
this and our other publications. Please visit www.imagespublishing.com.

CONTENTS

ALICE HOUSE

LONDON, UK
Spread Design

The Alice House environment encompasses all aspects of the area—a daytime family venue, a midday chill-out lunch space, and a night-time place to be seen in. The designers took the building back to its bare brick to expose its original beauty. By adding paneling to the walls and central bar the designers were able to contain the hand-painted graphics, which encompass the brand's look and feel. A design priority was to mix the old with the new. For instance, touches of humor and drama were added into the "old" style light bulbs by over-accentuating the original black-cord cabling that feeds back over the bar area.

Personal spaces were created within the bar by adding numerous sets of furniture styles and accessories, all of which were found in antique shops from around the UK. A front terrace allows patrons to soak in the local atmosphere.

1   Front terrace
2   Bar

1

3

4

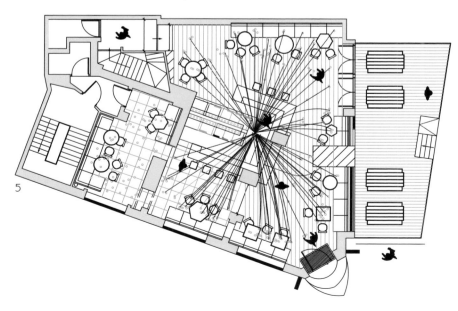

5

6

3   Bare brick walls show off the bar's
    original beauty

4   The design mixes the old with the new

5   Floor plan

6   Black-cord cabling feeds back over
    the bar

7   The wall paneling contains hand-
    painted graphics

Photography by Alastair Lever

aNISE BAR

LONDON, UK
B3 Designers

anise Bar is situated within the Cinnamon Kitchen, the sister restaurant to the famous Cinnamon Club in Westminster, London. Located in a former warehouse of the East India Trading Company, the design of the 2,500-square-foot bar is a result of a union between industrial heritage and the intricate, delicate detailing so abundant in Indian culture. Patrons are greeted by a patterned wall of mother-of-pearl mosaic tiles inspired by the geometrical and the floral patterns that form such a large part of traditional Indian arts. This geometric theme is continued in the hexagonal colored cement tiles that pave the floor.

Warm and distinctive sheesham wood is used throughout the space, alongside polished pewter and white-and-black marble. The muted color palette allows each of these rich materials to show off their inherent properties, which are complemented by silver-plated, perforated handmade lamps that throw dappled shadows onto interior surfaces, which are in turn reflected in the angled mirrors that line the walls. Within the main dining space, the Indian grill is made from black marble and polished pewter and allows customers to watch head chef Vivek Singh as he creates his famous signature dishes. Anise Bar is renowned for serving delicious cocktails, such as the signature Cinnamon Bellini, in an intricately designed and sophisticated environment.

1

1   Handmade lamp

2   A geometric theme is carried throughout the bar

2

4

3

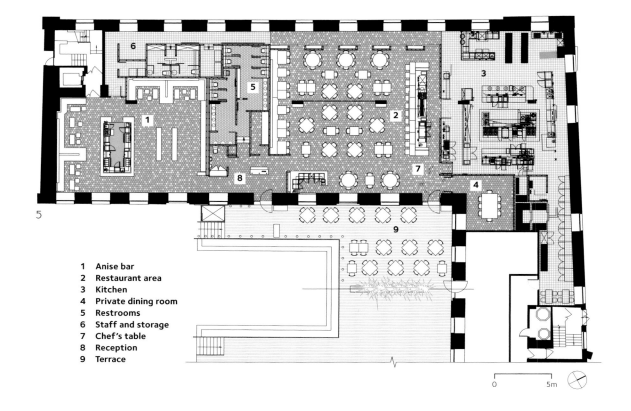

5

1 Anise bar
2 Restaurant area
3 Kitchen
4 Private dining room
5 Restrooms
6 Staff and storage
7 Chef's table
8 Reception
9 Terrace

3 & 4 Bar

5 Floor plan

6 Angled mirrors line the walls

7 The patterned wall greets patrons

Photography by Sean Pines

0   5m

6

7

aPOTHÉKE

NEW YORK CITY, NEW YORK, USA
Albert Trummer

1

inspired by the history and rise of the apothecary in Europe, as well as the artistic influence of absinthe dens in 19th-century Paris, Apothéke is a one-of-a-kind venue. The entire experience, from wandering down a hidden street to find the entrance to tasting the first sip of a specialty cocktail infused with exotic herbs and fruits, is an entirely unique experience.

Apothéke is based on the concept of an older-style Austrian apothecary from owner and master apothéker Albert Trummer's hometown in Vienna. Turn-of-the century apothecaries were originally created and designed to service kings and royalty due to the exclusiveness of remedies and medicinal treatments. Trummer has brought the atmosphere of traditional Eastern Europe to New York City with this modern day medicinal cocktail lounge, blending the old with the new for the future.

Trummer believes that the presentation of a cocktail should be just as dramatic as the cocktail itself, and Apothéke is more than a bar—it's a stage, a chemistry lab, and a theater. Trummer throws liquid fire from flasks, cuts Champagne bottles open with antique sabers, and has compiled unique, Austrian crystal glassware carefully chosen for individual cocktails. Far more than a simple cocktail bar, this venue is a cocktail apothecary.

1   Wandering down a hidden street to find the entrance is part of the experience

2–4   The bar is based on an older style Austrian apothecary

2

3

4

5

9

6

7

8

5   Apothéke is as much a chemistry lab as it is a bar

6   Owner Albert Trummer throws liquid fire from flasks

7 & 8   Drinks are made with exotic herbs and fruits

9 & 10   This modern day medicinal cocktail lounge blends the old with the new

Photography by Thomas Schauer

THE AVALON

LONDON, UK
Concorde BGW

Taking design cues from the heady days of the Victorian empire, The Avalon, named after the mythical island at the heart of the legend of King Arthur, mixes elements of a traditional tavern with the industrial and the luxurious, thanks to a successful collaboration between Tom Peake, artist Adam Ellis, Concorde BGW, and interior designer Hannah Lindsay. The striking highlight of the split-level bar area is the bespoke hand-colored wallpaper created by fusing together a number of Sir Edward Coley Burne-Jones (1833–98) paintings, including "The Last Sleep of King Arthur."

Swathed in light by four large bay windows, each decorated with unique asymmetric curtains, the room features a new 50-foot-long walnut bar accentuated by copper lamps, antique-white crackled-glazed tiles, original floor boards, two recently unearthed Victorian fireplaces, an olive-velvet chaise and chocolate Van Der Hoe chairs. The equally stylish adjoining dining room is marked by 10-foot-wide male and female chandeliers created by award-winning designer Jericho Hands using reclaimed parts of naval ships from the time when England ruled the waves. A bespoke 17-foot-wide wrought-iron mirror punctuates the end of the room, which also features a silver ceiling, mahogany display cabinets filled with antique spirits-and-beer bottles, as well as tiled walls imaginatively inlaid with illustrations from the 1853 editions of the *Illustrated London News*.

1   Detail of 17-foot-wide wrought-iron mirror

2   Copper lamps accentuate the walnut bar

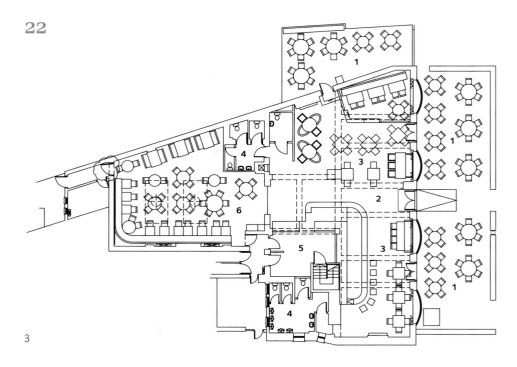

3

1 Garden
2 Entry
3 Bar
4 Restrooms
5 Store room
6 Restaurant

3 Floor plan

4 Illustrations are from 1853 editions of the *Illustrated London News*

5 The wallpaper depicts painting s by Sir Edward Coley Burne-Jones

6 Mahogany cabinets display antique bottles

7 Detail of the bar

Photography by Adam Ellis

4

5

6

7

bABEL

B3 Designers

1

The design inspiration for this 3,000-square-foot bar was found in the legendary Tower of Babel and its confusion of languages. Drawing on this concept, the designers created a confusion of visual styles that is found throughout the venue. In order to create a mixture of visual styles, each small detail of this project, including the mirrors, lights, furniture, and letters, was either custom-made or individually sourced. The eclectic visual style is achieved by incorporating different styles from different eras, for example 1950s-style furniture alongside a reclaimed 19th-century bar, complemented by contemporary lighting from individually sourced lampshades hanging over the main space.

Some of the light shades of this central lighting feature were made by the designers and covered with fabrics and tassels. The main feature wall comprises reclaimed letters, sourced from different salvage yards and a local store. Behind the bar sits a wall filled with small, framed mirrors that break up reflected images in a continuation of the "confusion" theme. Much time and effort was put into sourcing and creating unique and interesting fixtures and fittings, affording the venue a high degree of individuality.

1   The Tower of Babel was the inspiration for the interior design
2   The design concept is based on a confusion of visual styles
3   Babel exterior
4   A feature wall comprising reclaimed letters

2

3

4

5

5 Small framed mirrors fill the wall behind the bar

6 General view of interior

7 Lampshades were individually sourced

8 Floor plan

9 & 10 Interesting fixtures and fittings are a feature of the bar

Photography by Sean Pines

6

7

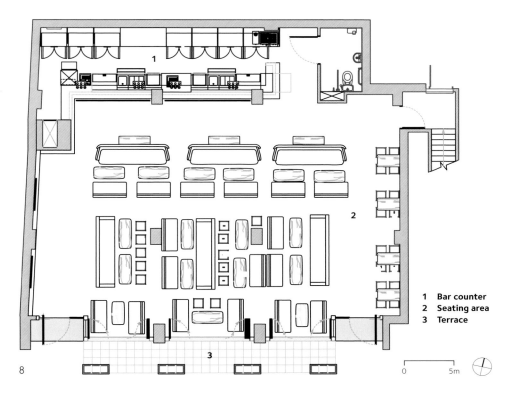

1   Bar counter
2   Seating area
3   Terrace

8

3

0   5m

9

10

bARBIE CAFÉ AND B-BAR

SHANGHAI, CHINA
Slade Architecture

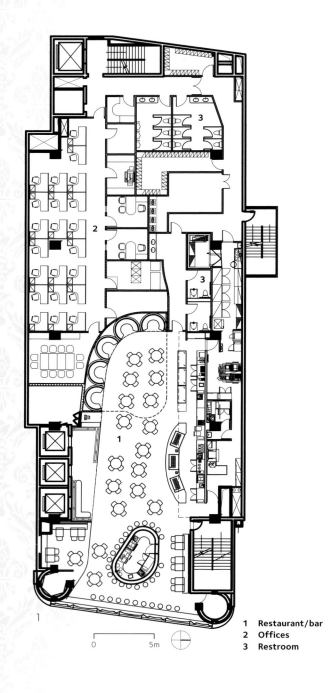

1   **Restaurant/bar**
2   **Offices**
3   **Restroom**

ocated on the sixth floor of the Barbie flagship store in Shanghai, China, the Barbie Café and B-Bar is an immersive experience intended to expand on the overall Barbie flagship store experience. Mattel worked with Shanghai-based celebrity chef-restaurateur David Laris to conceive a venue where European glamour meets classic American diner—a concept that expresses Barbie's international credentials and her American/Californian heritage.

By day, Barbie Café provides the perfect place for a refined meal, but at night B-Bar, a sculptural black bar under a hanging mobile of Barbie icon cut-outs, is open until late, serving an alluring menu of creative cocktails—such as BarbieTinis and Malibu Barbies—to real-life glamour girls and their attendant Kens. To accommodate the different ages and atmospheres, the architect chose a simple and striking palette—black lacquer, white accents, pink upholstery, and curtains—and the custom herringbone tile pattern on the floors and walls recalls the pattern of the swimsuit that Barbie first wore when she debuted at the New York Toy Fair in 1959.

The furniture, which was also designed by the architect, includes acrylic chairs printed with whimsical silhouette prints of iconic chairs—a combination of Chinese antique, European antique, and international modern—and the table bases are flat cut-out silhouettes of classic turned-wood profiles that continue the dialog between two-dimensional flat silhouette and three-dimensional objects. The furniture is a playful allusion to the Barbie Dreamhouse and other Barbie accessories, which use flat graphics to represent realistic detail at toy scale.

2

1   Floor plan

2 & 3   A restaurant by day and a bar by night, this venue expands on the overall Barbie flagship store experience

Photography by Iwan Baan and Mattel

3

bED

BIRMINGHAM, UK
Matt Rawlinson Design Ltd

Bed is a 550-capacity late bar comprising a large, full-length cocktail bar, lounge areas, and a dance floor with a DJ booth. The visual scheme is dark and decadent, featuring rich, candlelit oil paintings, drapes, and overstuffed furniture contrasted with graffiti and stencil art, broken mosaic, reclaimed timber, and deluxe junk.

The interior design was conceived as a piece of living street art. The entire area was sprayed in a dark graphite base color then covered with a mixture of stencil art, color splashes, and dribbled paintwork with tagging to give the spaces an urban back-street Italian aesthetic. A variety of walls feature free-form paint work, with individual classical style portraits worked into the scheme in specific areas and highlighted with carved black-lacquered frames. The interior has vast swagged drapes and velvet upholstery that is bleached in sections to add drama. In contrast, the furniture is modern British in style, with references to classic Chesterfields and 1960s chairs in a mixture of leathers and velvets.

The visual theme of Bed incorporates bric-à-brac furnishings and interior detailing, including oversized urns and candlebra, parlor palms, wall-mounted black church-style candles, oil paintings, frames, mirrors, statuary, antique reproduction sideboards and side tables, recycled dining chairs, high chairs, and poseur tables.

1 Overstuffed furniture is contrasted with graffiti
2 The full-length cocktail bar
3 Detail view of the bar

3

2

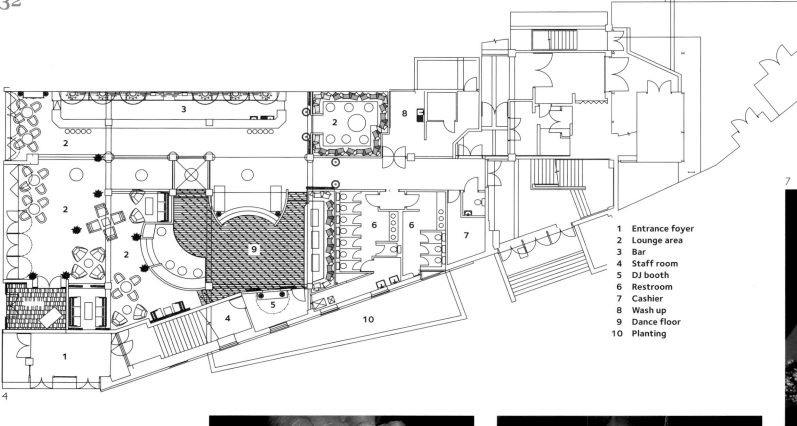

1 Entrance foyer
2 Lounge area
3 Bar
4 Staff room
5 DJ booth
6 Restroom
7 Cashier
8 Wash up
9 Dance floor
10 Planting

4

7

5

6

4 Floor plan

5 Carved black-lacquered frames highlight the space

6 Swagged drapes and velvet upholstery add drama

7 The interior design was conceived as a piece of living street art

Photography by Richard Southall @ Emphasis

THE BOTANIST

LONDON, UK
Laura Van Zeveren and Adam Ellis

1

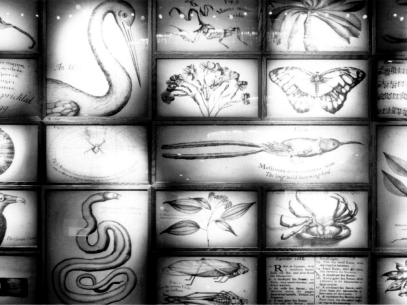

2

The key design feature as you enter The Botanist is the bespoke polished pewter bar which, along with the mirrored back bar and pewter tables, were produced by Benchmark Furniture, in collaboration with the interior designer. The exclusive touch continues with the circular, dark chocolate armchairs and is complemented by barstools in mustard leather. Hardwearing and yet elegant with its unvarnished finish, the flooring is hand-planed, pre-shrunk oak. A mirror designed to echo the chevron pattern of the floor provides the backdrop to the room, which is overseen by a portrait of Sir Hans Sloane, pioneering naturalist and Chelsea Physic Garden benefactor.

The centerpiece of the light and airy dining room is a collation of natural wonders, presented as a collector's cabinet of curiosities. During his research for the project, Adam Ellis unearthed Sloane's 1696 catalog of discoveries made on his voyage to the West Indies and now held by The Natural History Museum. Ellis took illustrations of flora and fauna from this rare book, transferring colored versions onto glass panels, which are illuminated in dark oak frames. During the day, windows that run the full length of two walls take full advantage of the corner location, filling the striking restaurant with natural light, while nocturnal illumination is provided by a trio of Miguel Mila's glamorous Estadio chandeliers.

1   The polished pewter bar is a key design feature

2   The wall is a display of Sir Hans Sloane's rare illustrations

Opposite   Illumination in the dining room is provided by Estadio chandeliers

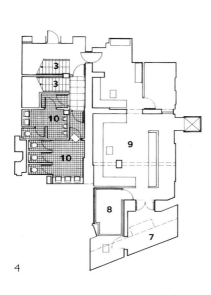
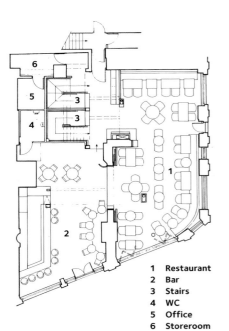

4

1 Restaurant
2 Bar
3 Stairs
4 WC
5 Office
6 Storeroom
7 Cellar
8 Cold room
9 Kitchen
10 Restrooms

5

4   Floor plans

5   The flooring is hand-planed, pre-shrunk oak

Opposite   The polished pewter bar

Photography by Richard Leeney

CAFÉ BAR M1

MUNICH, GERMANY
Atelier Brückner

1

The BMW Museum in Munich has a modern, dynamic language—the language of the automotive world. Opened in 2008, it sets a new standard in the realm of brand-focused museums. The designer has created an urban space with seven exhibition houses connected by streets, bridges, and squares. Each house has its own identity.

The Café Bar M1, located in the House of the Brand, is an integrative element of the museum. A continuous band element and an overhead light element conceptually link all rooms within the House of the Brand, which also accommodates the Museum Shop, a seminar room, and two exhibition rooms called Advertising: Reflecting the Times, and Encounters: Adventures and Experiences. BMW leather and Corian are the defining features of the bright, white bar design.

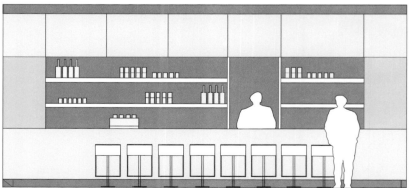

2

1 Focus on the main point of interest: overhead light element

2 Elevation

3 BMW leather and Corian are the defining features

3

4 Floor plan

5 Sitting at the bar: chairs aligned mirrored in Corian

6 A continuous band element made of BMW leather surrounds the guests

7 Overhead light element in detail: Corian as a defining feature

Photography by Marcus Meyer

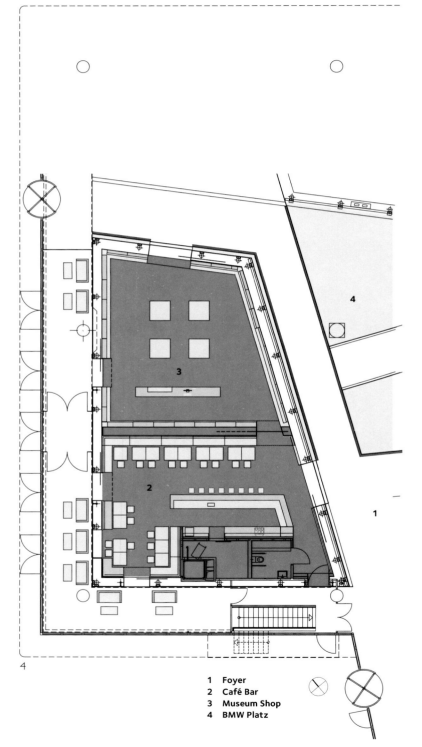

1 Foyer
2 Café Bar
3 Museum Shop
4 BMW Platz

5

6

7

CARBON BAR

LONDON, UK
B3 Designers

1

The interior of the 5,000-square-foot bar is a fusion of concrete, brick, steel, mesh, and leather. These rugged materials contrast against the inviting, outsized Chesterfields, beveled mirrors, and industrial-style sketches that pepper the walls. Elegantly architectural, the bar was designed to maximize space, privacy, and the ability to be seen from all areas. The venue has a 45-foot-long bar as well as a mezzanine Champagne bar, which hangs suspended over the lower ground floor. To access the mezzanine, patrons climb the stairs adjacent to a double-height Champagne wall filled with some of Taittinger's most expensive and rare bottles, including the Comtes de Champagne.

The DJ booth occupies a prominent position above the bar, placing the DJ at eye level with Champagne-sipping guests on the mezzanine floor. The interior design also includes a "chain room," which features giant, fixed steel chains hanging from floor to ceiling, creating the effect of a room within the main bar area. VIPs inside the chain room can be seen from the outside but are separated from the main space.

1   The huge metal door exudes industrial glamour and sultry Shoreditch style

2   General view of stenciled graffiti wall, main bar area, and DJ booth

3   Ground floor

4   A mezzanine champagne bar with two-story champagne wall and oversized Chesterfields

2

3

4

5

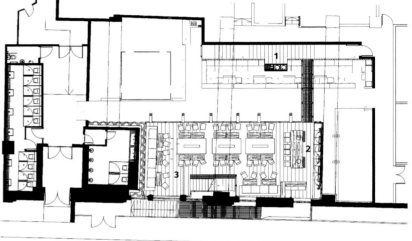

6

1 DJ area
2 Bar counter
3 Seating area

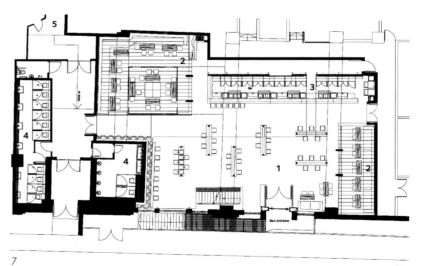

7

1 High tables and stools
2 Lounge area
3 Bar counter
4 Restrooms
5 Entry from hotel

0   6m

Photography by Sean Pines

8

CARGO BAR

HOBART, TASMANIA, AUSTRALIA
Paul Kelly Design

1

The design of this wine and pizza bar is based around a classic heritage-style interior with a raw/stripped concept balancing out the charm. The internal space features a large bar area, a high-bar standing area, raised side and rear lounges, and wide outdoor tables extending onto the street. The pizza kitchen can be viewed from the raised lounge. Wide openings allow natural light to spill through the space down to the street.

The fit out of the bar is designed to make it look as if it has been around since the 1800s, but all of the original elements were imported to give it that lived in feel. For example, to help make the interior look more original, handmade convict bricks were taken from a demolished 19th-century building and used to create the interior walls. The heritage look is contrasted by the use of raw steel mixed with white. For instance, the back-of-bar shelving unit is a continual piece of steel section bolted into the wall (with hidden LED lighting). The bar is made of steel profiles, all distressed with the addition of an antique mirror, which helps to maximize the depth of the room.

The main feature of the room is the diving spine wall, which divided the two original tenancies. Covered in white tiles, each tile laid in a different direction, it has the appearance of the original wall. However, with the benefit of lighting, the tile pattern shows different shapes in the shadowing. The raised lounge area, hidden between the recesses in the white-tiled wall, is a great place for customers to enjoy a glass of wine on the leather banquettes with the custom-designed acrylic pendants above.

1 & 3 The raised lounge area
2 & 4 The bar

2

3

4

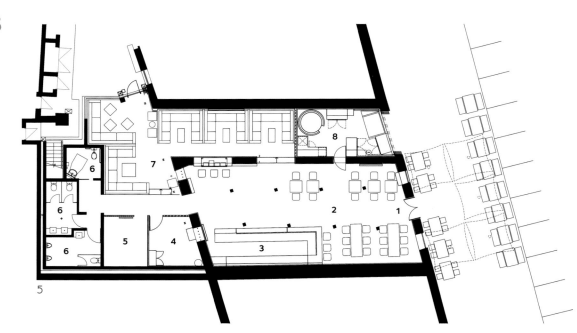

5

Photography by Sean Fennessy

1   **Entry**
2   **High seating area**
3   **Bar**
4   **Store room**
5   **Cool room**
6   **Restrooms**
7   **Lounge**
8   **Pizza kitchen**

6

7

8

9

10

11

tHE CASCADE ROOM

VANCOUVER, BRITISH COLUMBIA, CANADA
Evoke International Design Inc.

the Cascade Room is a 100-seat, 2,700-square-foot bar and restaurant that references traditional British pub design. The space unites a variety of organic materials with minimal, striking furnishings, and the overall ambience is achieved with carefully designed lighting and selected graphics. The main entrance to the venue is flanked by large overhead glass doors that open up to reveal the front lounge space and provide a strong connection between exterior and interior.

Inside, the main room is dominated by a 24-foot-long bar of reclaimed edge-grain pine that connects the raised dining areas near the front to the semi-private dining lounge toward the kitchen. Dark woods and built-in furnishings throughout create a casual, yet intimate experience regardless of the time of day. The back dining lounge provides a punch of warm color with a patchwork of burgundy, reds, and gold-flecked wallpaper, which has the effect of drawing patrons deeper into the room.

1   Booth seating

2   Semi-private area and window through to kitchen

3   Entrance

1

2

3

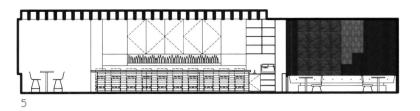

5

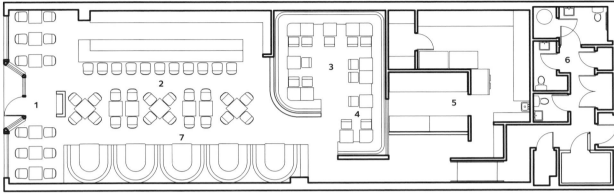

6

1 Entry
2 Main room
3 Semi-private area
4 Semi-private area with window through
  to kitchen
5 Kitchen
6 Restrooms
7 Booth seating and Queen Victoria lampshades

0   20ft

7

4 Queen Victoria lamp shades

5 Bar elevation

6 Floor plan

7 Semi-private area

Photography by Janis Nicolay

CASTLE HILL GREATER UNION GOLD CLASS CINEMA LOUNGE

SYDNEY, NEW SOUTH WALES, AUSTRALIA
Indyk Architects Pty Ltd

The intent of the design for this cinema lounge was to create mystery, delight and inventiveness, elements with which cinema is synonymous. The architects worked closely with the lighting designers, Point of View, to integrate seamlessly the lighting effects with joinery elements and architectural features. The form and arabesque of actual film, looped and ribboned through space, became a generating force.

This shaping is apparent in three-dimensional form. Space and height are divided by a strong ribbon-like element that forms a bulkhead through the space, defining and contrasting a 15-foot-high foyer space incorporating the Foyer Bar and Lit Pole Lounge with the 8-foot-high Ribbon Banquette Lounge. The bulkhead is composed of vertical acrylic boxes filled with film and backlit to create what is at once elusive, filmic, and lacelike. The Ribbon Banquette Lounge outline is conceal-lit by continuous cold-cathode neon lights built into the top of the joinery walls. The ribbon line invites and leads patrons into the lounge areas.

In direct contrast, the Lit Pole Lounge is lofty in height and moody in its color tones and acrylic poles. Fabric has been encircled within the acrylic hollow poles, which are lit top and bottom. An acoustic curved back wall helps to soften the space.

1   Mystery, delight, and inventiveness are the concepts driving the design
    of this cinema lounge

2   Foyer Bar

3 & 4   Lit Pole Lounge

2

3

4

5

6

7

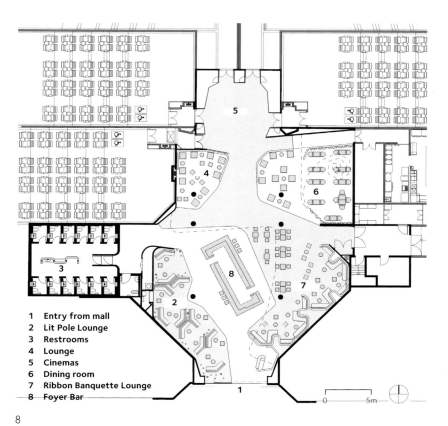

1 Entry from mall
2 Lit Pole Lounge
3 Restrooms
4 Lounge
5 Cinemas
6 Dining room
7 Ribbon Banquette Lounge
8 Foyer Bar

0 — 5m

8

5 The lighting effects have been seamlessly integrated throughout the lounge

6 & 7 The Ribbon Banquette Lounge outline is conceal-lit by continuous cold-cathode neon lights

8 Floor plan

9 Restroom

10 Detail of the tiled wall of individual toilets, tiles, and Corian light box

Photography by Richard Weinstein

9

10

CHANDELIER ROOM

HOBOKEN, NEW JERSEY, USA
ICRAVE

1

The Chandelier Room is a warm and comfortable lounge designed to become the social hub and energy source for the W Hoboken Hotel. The space is blessed with classic proportions, river views, and an expansive terrace—three key ingredients for an archetypal "great room." In the design treatment, these views have been artfully concealed and revealed to become part of the architecture itself. The space's colors and textures are rich and warm—copper tiles, glazed cognac leathers, and chocolate velvets are used extensively—and the bar's heady tortoise tones are cut through with absinthe-colored accents that give it a distinctive edge and energy.

Taking center stage, however, is a remarkable chandelier to end all chandeliers—a glossy and glamorous fixture, oversized and scaled to fantastic proportions. Like something from a fantasy dollhouse, this astonishing piece cascades down from the ceiling to become a playful and inhabitable sculpture that captures the impressive height of the room. The chandelier engages, masks, and flirts, and guests can actually sit in the crystal drop chairs that appear to hang from its merlot-colored boughs. This unique structure is the defining element of the space—grand in proportion, warm and whimsical, and unquestionably sexy.

1   The chandelier to end all chandeliers
2   The lounge's plush seating offers spectacular views of the Manhattan skyline

2

3

4

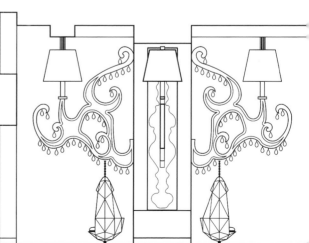

5

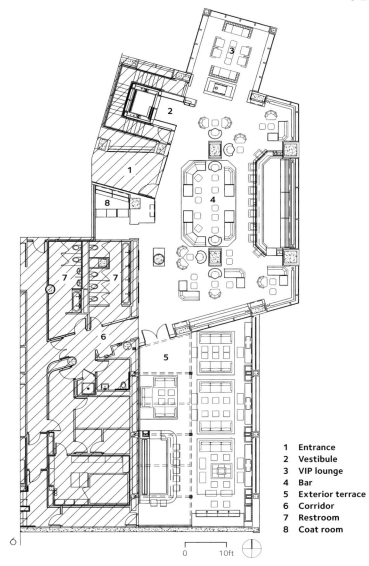

1 Entrance
2 Vestibule
3 VIP lounge
4 Bar
5 Exterior terrace
6 Corridor
7 Restroom
8 Coat room

0   10ft

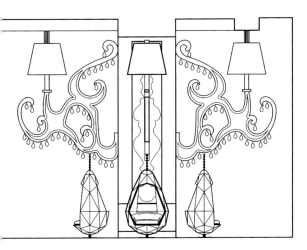

3   The fireplace conceals a more private space beyond

4   Views of the Manhattan skyline are a part of the architecture

5   Detail drawing of the chandelier

6   Floor plan

Photography by John Bartelstone

CLOUDLAND

BRISBANE, QUEENSLAND, AUSTRALIA
Felix Minturn

Spanning four levels, with a retractable glass roof that opens with the touch of a button, Cloudland is designed to be a veritable urban oasis. Although the idea of an open-air venue is far from new, Cloudland couldn't be further removed from your average corner-hotel beer garden. Springing from designer Nic Brunner's vivid imagination, Cloudland is more like a film set for a futuristic Garden of Eden that just happens to operate as a combination bar, restaurant, and function space.

The venue has been designed to be visually stunning. There are 5,000 plants climbing and sprawling over a 46-foot interior wall set off by a 33-foot waterfall. A touch of elegance is brought into the garden by way of two bars, one made from solid hand-carved China-white marble and the other made from 19,000 glass balls threaded together by hand.

Cloudland effortlessly transcends eras, clichés, and standard hospitality architectural guidelines. It has been transformed from what was essentially a spare lot into a fantastical bar and restaurant, the likes of which has never been seen in Brisbane. Its concepts and inspirations are many and varied from open tree-top watering holes in the jungles of South America, to the pulsing beat of a chic Parisian discotheque; Cloudland is an unexplicable yet delightful fusion of cultures and customs.

1

1   Entrance to Cloudland

2   Japanese style booths provide another way to dine beneath the clouds

3

3   The glass-ball bar and patent-leather booths in the Crystal Palais

4   Take a seat in the Crystal Palais

5   Persian booths located in the Crystal Palais on the mezzanine level

6   The wrought-iron furniture in the dining area provides a whimsical take on the traditional garden setting

7   The women's restrooms on the ground floor offer a rosy glow

Photography by Kylie Hood

4

5

6

7

CLOVER CLUB

NEW YORK CITY, NEW YORK, USA

Michael Brais, Susan Fedroff, and Julie Reiner

1

With an extensive list of handcrafted classic cocktails and an opulent, Victorian-inspired interior, Clover Club offers a 78-seat lounge and private back parlor for up to 40 guests. Named after the infamous Philadelphia 1920s literary hangout, this bar is a stylish haunt celebrating the craft of the cocktail. The Victorian-inspired décor of this expansive space is sumptuous and inviting. Tin ceilings, lanterns, mosaic tiles, dark mahogany wood, antique sconces, luxe wall coverings, and a massive antique bar contribute to the refined elegance of the interior. The venue is divided into two separate rooms, with a bar in each area.

Clover Club's focal point is a brilliantly restored mahogany wood bar circa 1892, which was salvaged from a house in an old coal mining town in Pennsylvania. The magnificent bar is accented by deluxe overstuffed barstools, designed for guests to stay awhile. The back room is decked out in velvety Victorian parlor furniture and features an elegant marble fireplace. With seating for 30, this is a cozy space where guests can enjoy a more intimate cocktail-bar experience. Special features of this area include a cocktail list offering selections from the main cocktail menu along with an expansive library of cocktail recipes compiled over the years. All drinks here are served in vintage glassware that the owner has collected over several decades. The back room is also designed for private parties, educational seminars, and to host guest bartenders.

1   Handcrafted classic cocktails in vintage glassware are the house speciality

2   The restored mahogany bar, circa 1892

3

3   The back room features an elegant marble fireplace

4 & 7   Deluxe overstuffed barstools and booths are designed for guests
       to stay awhile

5 & 6   Victorian-inspired details such as these add to the refined elegance
       of the interior

Photography by Oleg March

5

6

4

7

COMME

MELBOURNE, VICTORIA, AUSTRALIA
Hecker Phelan Guthrie

1

Comme is a unique venue that offers a range of beautifully designed drinking, dining, and event spaces. The task of transforming the existing 1885 building into a modern destination was a challenge welcomed by the owners. The driving philosophy was to retain the building's Victorian heritage while creating a contemporary and exciting experience. The result is a sophisticated venue characterized by luxury, glamour, and elegance.

The Wine Room offers a stylish interior experience and is a space capable of accommodating a large crowd or providing an intimate experience during quieter times. The centrally located marble bar provides the main point of activity and is articulated by two large iconic Cocoon pendant lights. The wine pod feature to the rear of the bar acts as reserve wine storage and a unique display, as well as highlighting the extent of Comme's cellar.

The Grand Room, with its spectacular 20-foot-high ceilings and 3-foot-deep decorative cornices, is one of the most impressive spaces in the building. The decorative Victorian detail and interior has been retained with the insertion of a modern, freestanding marble bar located at the end of the room. While functioning as the workstation and focal point of the Grand Room, the bar has the ability to shut down and blend into the setting for more traditional events. Two contemporary green Murano glass chandeliers are the heroes of the space. Overtly glamorous and impressive in scale, these two chandeliers encapsulate the owner's vision for this room. The adjoining Onyx Room follows a similar design approach in relation to the black marble bar and furniture. Accommodating smaller groups and events, it offers a highly flexible space and a warm and inviting atmosphere.

1   View looking down to the wine pod

2 & 3   The 1885 building has been transformed into a modern destination

4   The Wine Room offers a warm and inviting atmosphere

2

3

4

6

5

7

8

5   The bar offers a warm and inviting atmosphere

6   The Grand Room

7   The Onyx Room

8   The intimate setting of Comme Kitchen

Photography by Earl Carter

CORPER BLEU

LAKEVILLE, MINNESOTA, USA
Jordan Mozer and Associates

1

This undulating copper-clad restaurant on the edge of Minneapolis has an interior entirely composed of wood and features natural regional materials, curves, and horizontal lines all illuminated by 25,000 glowing test tubes. The tilted bar wall features horizontal stripes of chocolate and blue glass mosaic tiles, and supports sculpted aluminum brackets topped with computer-milled milk-acrylic shelves displaying liquor and wine bottles. The bar is built of mahogany with a bartop surface of solid, oiled end-grain mesquite blocks. Cast-aluminum and blown-glass lamps sit on the bar.

Parallel to the bar is a long communal table also finished with blocks of mesquite and supported by a steel frame. In the middle of the table a long block of limestone supports a hand-made, cast-bronze candelabra filled with 20 candles. The stools in the bar, like the seating throughout, have the suggestion of wings. They are framed in dark wood and are upholstered in dark brown velvet.

1–4 The undulating copper-clad restaurant shines in the sunlight

2

3

4

5   The interior features natural regional materials

6   Floor plan

7   Sculpted aluminum brackets support acrylic shelves

8–10   The interior is entirely composed of wood

11   Cast aluminum and blown-glass lamps sit on the bar

Photography by Doug Snower

6

5

7

8

9

10

11

CROWN & SCEPTRE

ADELAIDE, SOUTH AUSTRALIA, AUSTRALIA
Grimaldi Architects

Known as Adelaide's bartenders' bar, the double-story Crown & Sceptre offers one of the largest and most comprehensive ranges of premium spirits and liqueurs in Australia, with more than 500 different products and a celebrated and innovative drinks list. The interior design was inspired by the owner's love of retro chic and 1960s and 70s style mixed in with a vibrant Pop Art splash of color. All areas were designed to promote a feeling of warmth and create an inviting atmosphere that encourages patrons to linger and enjoy the surrounds.

The renovation and fit out was sympathetic to the architecture of the original venue, which was built in 1873, but also incorporates fascinating design cues from pop culture, retro symbolism, and modern trends. Many of the interior features of the bar are custom made, from the hand-mixed paints that were created on site to the artistic murals and locally designed lighting fixtures. The Sceptre is an institution on the Adelaide scene and the highly awarded mixologists are a great source of entertainment as they whip up signature drinks and cocktails with flair and expertise.

1   Just some of the 500 products on offer
2   Detail view of the bar
3   Ground floor plan
4   The bar

1

2

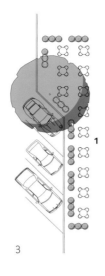

3

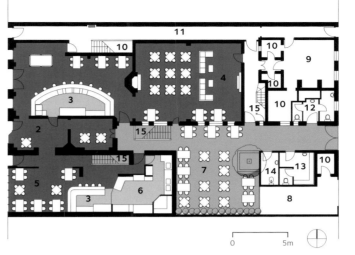

1. Outdoor dining
2. Entry hall
3. Bar
4. Lounge
5. Dining
6. Kitchen
7. Courtyard
8. Service yard
9. Dry store
10. Store room
11. Staff corridor
12. Women's restroom
13. Men's restroom
14. Access restroom
15. Stairs

0   5m

4

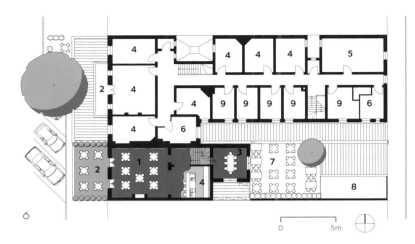

1   Dining
2   Balcony
3   Courtroom 32 bar
4   Office
5   Staff area
6   Restroom
7   Courtyard below
8   Service yard below
9   Store room

6

5

7

5   Artistic murals cover many of the walls

6   First floor

7   Lighting fixtures were locally designed

8   All areas are designed to be warm and inviting

9   Many of the interior features of the bar are custom made

Photography by Ben Macmahon

8

9

CROWNE PLAZA

QUEENSTOWN, NEW ZEALAND
Dalman Architecture

When this property was upgraded, an extended restaurant and bar and several retail spaces were added, improving the urban presence of the hotel. It was a conscious design decision to allow a series of moods and subspaces within the lobby-reception-bar areas. There is an open and flowing relationship between bar, lobby, reception, and restaurant. These interrelated spaces form the overall atmosphere of the public experience of entering the hotel. However, the restaurant and bar are still visible from the hotel lobby with easy access from the lifts to ensure house guests are not forgotten about.

The bar space had to be fitted around a number of structural walls. This has been used to the bar's advantage by separating a number of bar seating areas, each with their own characteristics to suit different moods. The Martini Bar is a small, dark space discreetly nestled behind fabric-lined paddle doors. The polished black-granite bar front continues onto the floor then folds up the opposite wall. An internally lit, wiggly glass bench with acrylic stools continues the hard and shiny theme. This is contrasted with deep-red velvet drapes, and softened acoustically by perforated ply ceiling tiles. The shiny surfaces reflect the changing colors of the light wall at the rear of the bar. The Glass Bar is brighter and features glass art from New Zealand's top glass artists. The Bed Bar is an informal relaxed area great for après-ski socializing. Guests climb up onto the large divan and snuggle into throw cushions.

1 Detail of one of the tables
2 View toward the bar from the hotel reception
3 View from the entrance toward the bed bar
4 Meths fires separate the bar from the hotel lobby

2

3

4

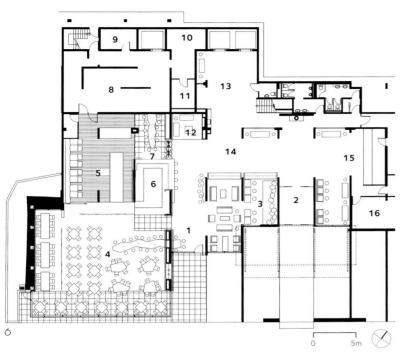

6

1 Entry
2 Wind lobby
3 Bed Bar
4 threesixty restaurant
5 Buffet
6 Bar
7 Martini Bar
8 Kitchen
9 Cold store
10 Food & beverage manager/store
11 Chef
12 Glass Bar
13 Lobby
14 Foyer
15 Reception
16 Luggage room

0   5m

8

9

7

10

Cumberland Club's Chamberlain Bar

PORTLAND, MAINE, USA
Barba + Wheelock

Located in central Portland, the club occupies a 1802 Federal-style house. Steeped in history, the Cumberland Club was looking to update its staid image with a new gathering space central to the operations: a bar that was traditional in style and yet innovative in its design. The bar's location is adjacent to the U.S.S Maine Room, a dark-wooded room lined with lockers replete with a two-toned striped wood floor. The new bar transformed the tired interior of an adjacent room into a comfortable wood-lined extension. A key challenge to overcome in the planning was the design of the back bar that integrated a very sophisticated set of kitchen/bar equipment in a limited amount of space.

Two different species of wood were selected for the striped floor for their inherent characteristics to allow for a one-step process of clear finish. The granite countertop picked up the tonal quality of the room in a permanent and utilitarian surface. The German-made glass is translucent enough to allow views out from the room to a hint of the green landscape beyond, but textured to disguise the identity of nearby diners. The lead pattern is modeled on the historic windows in the adjacent Maine Room. Daylight filters in though the glass wall, illuminating bottles and glassware; concealed specialty lighting augments the natural light providing a sparkle to the bar.

1   A view into the bar from the U.S.S. Maine Room
2   Floor plan
3   The bar
4   The bar highlighting the striped wood floor
5   The granite countertop picks up the tonal quality of the room

Photography by Sandy Agrafiotis

1

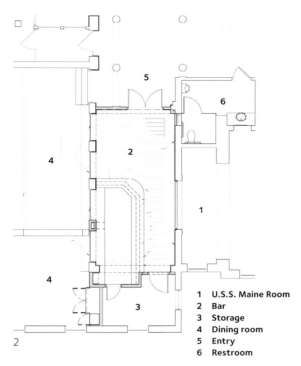

1 U.S.S. Maine Room
2 Bar
3 Storage
4 Dining room
5 Entry
6 Restroom

2

3

4

5

CUTLER & CO. DINING ROOM AND BAR

MELBOURNE, VICTORIA, AUSTRALIA
Pascale Gomes-McNabb

designer Pascale Gomes-McNabb has created a restaurant and bar that achieves balance between the varied layers of service, function, comfort, and pleasure with a series of finely detailed elements set against a rough shell of a former metalwork factory. The glass street frontage, opaque by day, becomes luminous at night revealing the unfolding theater of a restaurant in operation.

The monolithic black-metal bar acts as a battlement to the restaurant proper; a perforated up-lit liquor shelf hovers like a forest canopy above. A black service spine contains the glass candy box wine store, the "Scarface" smoke-and-mirror booth, glass automatic doors that flash glimpses of the acid-yellow kitchen, and within a black "outhouse" are jewel-colored toilet compartments.

Long gray-leather banquettes unify and reinforce the linearity of the space floating over the herringbone parquet floor. On the rough brick wall, erratically placed smoky mirrors reflect a series of vignettes. The palette of dark tones and colors alludes to intrigue and luxury that marries with the product on offer. The cloud light designed specifically for the space hovers playfully over diners, creating a fun environment.

1 The black-metal bar

2 Façade at night

3 The venue is set within an old metal-work factory

4 View looking down to the bar

2

3

4

5   Long banquettes unify the linearity of the space

6   A series of Robert Owen sculptures decorate the walls

7   Floor plan

8 & 9   The palette of dark tones and colors alludes to intrigue and luxury

Photography by Peter Bennetts

6

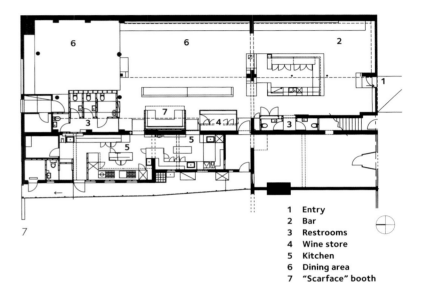

7

1   **Entry**
2   **Bar**
3   **Restrooms**
4   **Wine store**
5   **Kitchen**
6   **Dining area**
7   **"Scarface" booth**

8

9

DIAMOND BAR

CHRISTCHURCH, NEW ZEALAND
Dalman Architecture

The Christchurch Casino building was built to an overall "volcanic" design concept, with the Diamond Bar located deep within. Presented with a brief to create a bar that offers a unique experience for patrons, the architect decided to develop the bar's location and used the unexposed, concealed nature of the space to create a hidden jewel—an area that, once found, leads you on a journey deeper into the heart of the "volcano." This concept is reflected within both the furnishings and layout of the bar.

Upon entering, patrons find themselves in a glamorous, comfortable lounge area with chandeliers centered over large leather seats, adjacent to 3,500 crystal-cut glass strands that are suspended over a clean white bar. As patrons venture deeper within the space the furnishings become more intense, with red-velvet walls and light reflections dancing off floating mirror panels. At the end of the journey through the bar is a welcoming fireplace, where a black-mosaic stage is surrounded with glowing wax candles.

By combining design features such as chandeliers, leather seats, velvet finishes, granite walls, feature LED lighting, and high-quality sound systems, an exciting infusion of new and old is created to achieve a sophisticated, intriguing, and welcoming bar.

1 & 2   The bar is a hidden jewel in the center of the casino

2

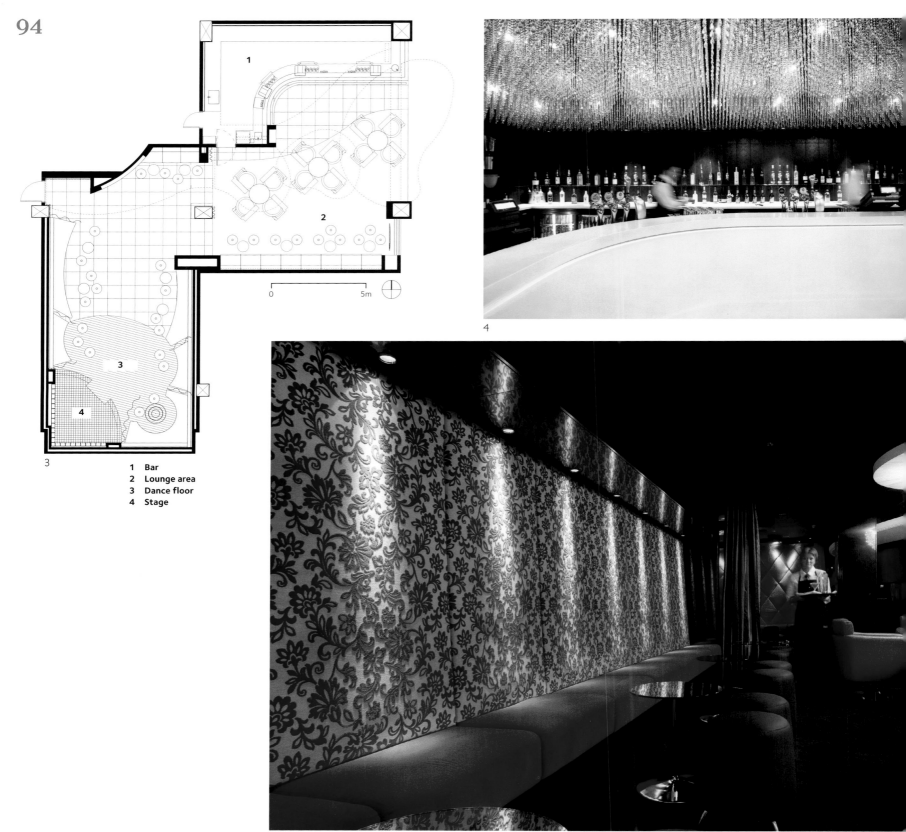

1 Bar
2 Lounge area
3 Dance floor
4 Stage

0   5m

3

4

5

3   Floor plan

4   Suspended over the bar are 3,500
    crystal-cut glass strands

5 & 6   Red-velvet walls and floating mirror
        panels are a feature of the bar

Photography by Stephen Goodenough

6

ELIZA'S WINE BAR

SANCTUARY COVE, QUEENSLAND, AUSTRALIA
coop creative

1

2

Situated at Sanctuary Cove on Queensland's Gold Coast, Eliza's was created to service a gaming room. The design of the bar challenges typical gaming-room aesthetic, as the intention was to provide a destination within the village that appeals to varying clientele, not only those wanting to gamble.

Typically, gaming rooms are loud and lairy with bold carpet and neon lights, a recipe that clearly works for this style of venue. However, the designers took this formula in the opposite direction to create an exciting and enticing space that has a separate identity to the gaming room. Drawing on the surrounding 1980s architecture found in the rest of the village, the designers created an entire space with movie-set styling not unlike the village itself. Though the gaming room was treated with minimal fuss in order to let it exists in its own right, the bar is heavily layered using color and detail. The result is a bar that is bright and cheery by day, and sophisticated and enticing by night.

1   External view of the wine bar showing the small scale of the space
2   Elevation of the bar with the gaming machines visible in the background
3   Floor plan
4   As the sun sets over the marina the bar takes on a warm and sophisticated appearance
5   The bold color is bright and cheery during the day
6   The interior detailing and bold wallpaper are enticing

Photography by Andrew Yeo

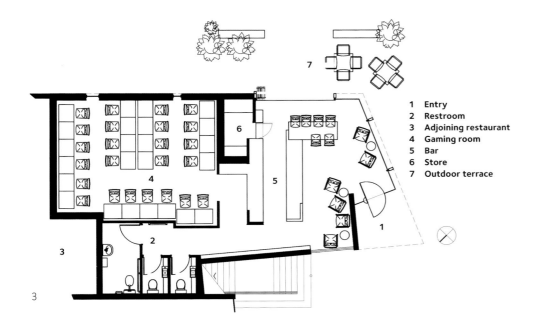

1 Entry
2 Restroom
3 Adjoining restaurant
4 Gaming room
5 Bar
6 Store
7 Outdoor terrace

3

5

4

6

EMPORIUM HOTEL COCKTAIL BAR

BRISBANE, QUEENSLAND, AUSTRALIA
Francine John with Greg Harris Design

a key design element used throughout the Emporium Hotel is the frangipani, and this motif is continued through to the cocktail bar in the form of two huge entry doors made of laser-cut stainless steel and glass. The bar itself is an eclectic fusion of styles—a combination of antique pieces from around the world, custom-made retro-look furniture, and an integrated digital audio-visual screen.

The design of the hotel was conceptualized and driven by owner Francine John, who created the overall concept, look and feel, inspired by the frangipani flower. Greg Harris Design worked closely with Francine in delivering her interior-design vision. The majority of the design features were sourced locally by Queensland-based artists and suppliers. However, in the cocktail bar, the grand onyx bar is lit by an antique German chandelier, originally from a castle in Europe that was home to elegant debutante balls. Another stunning feature of the bar is an exquisite stained-glass wall, originally a Parisian shopfront crafted more than 100 years ago. The piece was exported to Buenos Aires where it was used as a window in a mansion, before being flown to Australia by an antiques dealer, and catching the eye of the Emporium Hotel.

1   An antique German chandelier hangs above the grand onyx bar

2 & 3   The frangipani motif is used throughout the hotel, including the bar doors

1

2

3

4

5

6

4 & 5   The grand onyx bar

6   The stained-glass wall was originally part of a Parisian shopfront

8   Floor plan

7 & 9   The bar is an electic fusion of styles

Photography by Bill Watson

7

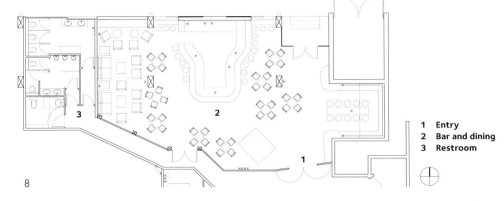

1   Entry
2   Bar and dining
3   Restroom

8

9

EUREKA 89

MELBOURNE, VICTORIA, AUSTRALIA
Maddison Architects

1

Located at the top of the Eureka Tower, and occupying a space originally designed for machinery and equipment, this bar has arguably the best views, and possibly the lowest ceilings, of any Melbourne venue. The architect was provided with a brief to design a self-contained facility that included seating for up to 150, a kitchen, a cocktail bar, and separate divisible spaces to cater for smaller groups, and which capitalized on and enhanced the views over the city.

To achieve this brief, the architect provided spaces that could be closed off with folding wall panels or gold chain-link operable curtains. When open, these devices allow a seamless, united space, and when closed create discrete intimate, individual spaces. At the city-view end an open floor plate with one large, seamless, timber-clad solid wall element also carries all the storage and back-of-house services. At the opposite end of the space, a cantilevered stone bar reflects the oblique geometry found in the Eureka building itself. Above the bar hangs a Swarovski, red LED-lit chandelier.

Vertical surfaces throughout are either charcoal or black, whether aluminum, glass, or carpet. The dominant feature is the perforated, acoustic metal ceiling, which is painted Ferrari red and uplit with red neon. The pattern from this perforated ceiling is derived from the pattern of the floor plan, and the floor plan geometry is again represented in the gold motif in the carpet, where the sinuous outline is repeated and is spun to form rosettes, much like those created by a "Spirograph" set. Red-leather parallelogram wall cladding, in either perforated or solid sheet, wraps the walls to the cocktail bar.

1   Bar view
2   Circulation space, through to bar

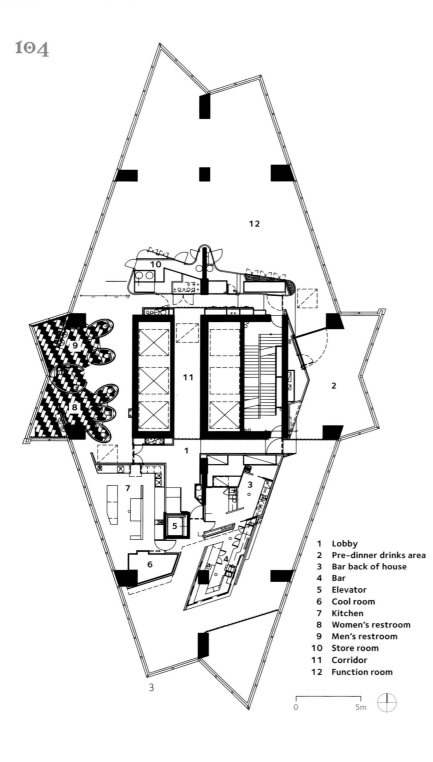

1 Lobby
2 Pre-dinner drinks area
3 Bar back of house
4 Bar
5 Elevator
6 Cool room
7 Kitchen
8 Women's restroom
9 Men's restroom
10 Store room
11 Corridor
12 Function room

0   5m

3 Floor plan

4 Function room

Photography by Rhiannon Slatter

4

FREAK BAR

BROOKLYN, NEW YORK, USA
Philip Tusa, Architect

1

Set in the historic 1917 Child's Surf Avenue Restaurant building, the Coney Island USA Freak Bar & Museum Gift Shop was most recently a US Army Recruiting Station. The project at hand was initiated when Coney Island USA (CIUSA) was awarded a grant to purchase the Child's Building. CIUSA is a not-for-profit arts organization that presents Sideshows by the Seashore, the only remaining "ten-in-one" live sideshow in Coney Island, as well as several other annual events. CIUSA rented part of the first-floor sideshow amusement arcade and the entire second floor housing the Coney Island Museum.

After inheriting the prominent Surf Avenue storefront spaces, the planning challenge was to incorporate the new spaces to connect to the existing spaces. The existing Freak Bar in the West 12th Street sideshow entry was expanded into the corner space and a new museum gift shop was relocated from upstairs to form a new museum entrance lobby on the sidewalk level. Together the new spaces form an interconnected whole that functions as CIUSA's "Front Door on Coney's Surf Avenue."

Architecturally, this transformation was achieved by perforating the existing dividing partitions with large-scale oculus and archway openings. Of historical note, hidden underneath aged plywood signs were the beautiful arches that were part of the historic façade; these are now revealed and incorporated in all their splendor. Decoratively, the "Coney-esque" style has been successfully employed. Historically CIUSA has sought to evoke an atmosphere that signifies the nostalgia that Coney is to all people worldwide, whether they remember it personally or have just heard of it. "Coney-esque" is colorful, bold, graphically abrasive, and is designed to be spectacular both night and day.

2

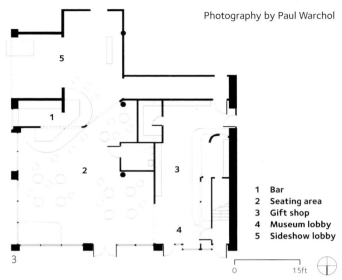

1 & 4 Bar
2 Exterior view
3 Floor plan
5 Museum lobby

Photography by Paul Warchol

1 Bar
2 Seating area
3 Gift shop
4 Museum lobby
5 Sideshow lobby

3

0   15ft

4

5

GAZEBO WINE GARDEN

SYDNEY, NEW SOUTH WALES, AUSTRALIA
Dale Jones-Evans Pty Ltd Architecture

1

The Gazebo Wine Garden is housed in the former Gazebo Hotel, a venue once infamous for its vivid and colorful social history. The bar is located adjacent to the equally interesting Fitzroy Gardens and a local square, its site buried in the middle of the nightclub and red-light district of Kings Cross.

The design for the 300-seat Gazebo Wine Garden fits into the existing circumferential space and uses artistic twists, the adjacent park, and the re-articulation of the former building's history in its interior design and fit out. Those contextual echoes of decadence, the down and out, and the gardens all resonate in a room full of wine—a cellar-type space where people can sit and engage with the sensual and whimsical interior.

The incorporation of art installations that play on history, sentiment, and curiosity create a psychological stage set of events, engineered to foster social interaction and open the familiar in unfamiliar ways. Many degrees of interactivity are embedded into the space, from the blackboard doors you can graffiti on in the mixed-gender toilet spaces, to the distinctive furniture.

The bar references the adjacent gardens through interior elements such as the live, wet moss wall behind the bar, the charcoal log-wall infused with simulacraic flora, and the stained moss-green plywood ceiling. Inventive use of inexpensive and recycled materials are intriguing interior features: the main chandelier comprises fishing lures and weights on fishing lines, while the hanging installations sit on repurposed pizza trays. Even the bar top is made from reclaimed timber. The feature charcoal wall was burnt in a crematorium, which was the only place that had a furnace big enough to handle the size of the logs.

1   Detail of veranda and garden terrace
2   Verdant shingled plywood ceiling pulls
    the external park into the bar

2

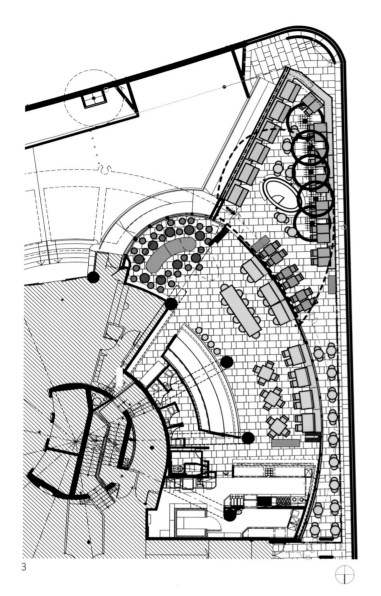

3

4

5

6

3   Floor plan

4   Recycled plywood, rusted reinforcement mesh wine display and old news-wallpaper

5   Live moss wall behind the bar

6   Rouge studded sofa, charcoal logs, and lead-weight chandelier

Photography by John Gollings

THE IRISH HEATHER

VANCOUVER, BRITISH COLUMBIA, CANADA
Evoke International Design Inc.

1

The 100-plus-seat Irish Heather gastro pub is located in a recently renovated heritage building in Vancouver's historic Gastown neighborhood. Patrons are welcomed into the main, open space by a large Waterford Crystal chandelier and a 33-foot-long wooden bar.

The flooring for the main room was sourced from 100-year-old reclaimed Guinness barrels, infusing this modern space with rustic elegance. Period Irish wallpaper adds accents, contrasting against the building's exposed brick walls. Although the room is open, it's also divided into snugs and railings that provide varying degrees of intimacy. A 40-foot-long fir beam, which originally served as a ceiling support, has found new life as the central, communal table. The kitchen and washroom area is clad in copper panels, chosen to patina with age, that display the symbol of the Irish boar.

The pub is connected to the proprietor's adjacent Salty Tongue Deli by a narrow washroom corridor, which also provides an overflow area at night. The design of The Irish Heather incorporates display areas to showcase the owner's extensive collection of Irish memorabilia, a passion reinforced through Irish poetry and quotes integrated on the restroom doors that are visible when illuminated from inside. The coach house at the back of the building houses the Shebeen Whisky House, which showcases British Columbia's finest collection of whisky.

2

3

4

1   Glass exterior

2   Entrance

3   Communal table

4   Drink rail

1 Glass exterior
2 Entry
3 Communal table
4 Drink rail
5 Copper cladding
6 Bar
7 Corridor through to communal table
8 Snug area
9 Restroom-door graphics
10 Restrooms
11 Shebeen Whisky House

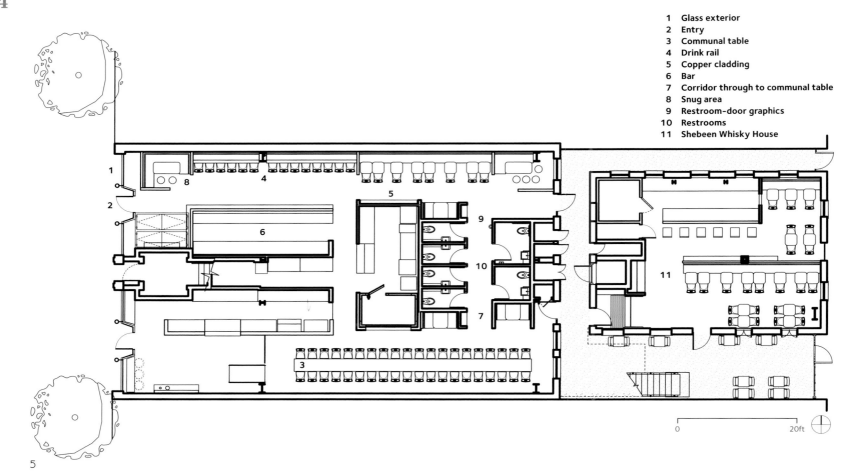

0   20ft

5

6

7

8

9

Photography by Janis Nicolay and The Irish Heather

10

LIBERTINE

BRISBANE, QUEENSLAND, AUSTRALIA
Arkhefield + Robert Douglas/Jamie Webb/Heath Williamson

1

Occupying key street frontage in the redevelopment of a derelict, heritage-listed barracks building that had sat vacant for 20 years, the collaboration between the designers, the client, and various craftspeople culminated in a sophisticated space that does justice to this unique and timeless venue.

Libertine's brief was to embrace a style that not only references and is respectful toward the history of the existing architecture, but also reclaims the site through a contemporary design and conceptual narrative. This attitude is manifest in the overlaying of the French Vietnamese flavor of rich, opulent layering of multiple wallpapers, specialty wall finishes, and salvaged chandeliers hung from richly colored recessed domes within the ceiling space.

Warm pools of light concentrated over individual tables enhance the dining experience and add to the intimate experience of the restaurant. Wall washing light fittings along the perimeter of the space provide an intimate, introverted light quality that heightens the feeling of color, texture, and space. The Libertine experience is a visceral one and intentionally so. The interior spaces mediate between calm, quiet, and introverted areas and larger, more social and extroverted spaces designed for gathering and meeting. This carefully designed venue meets the needs of a single couple or a group with equal attention to scale, experience, and quality.

1   The French Vietnamese branding forms the basis for the design methodology
Opposite   Collaboration with master craftsman gave a bespoke nature to joinery elements

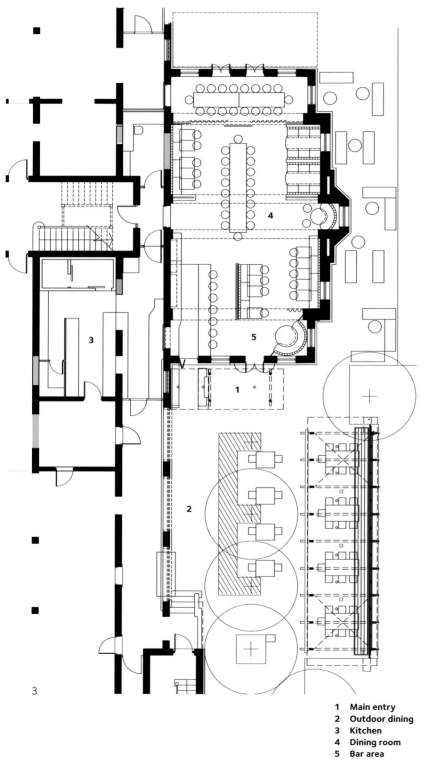

3

1 Main entry
2 Outdoor dining
3 Kitchen
4 Dining room
5 Bar area

4

5

7

6

3 Floor plan

4 A sophisticated space in a prime location

5 Spaces are defined by handmade screens

6 Existing timber doors, windows, architraves, and floors were all restored to their original state

7 Crafted pods create an environment as bespoke as the dining experience itself

Photography by Scott Burrows, Aperture Photography

LOCAL KITCHEN AND WINE MERCHANTS

SAN FRANCISCO, CALIFORNIA, USA
Sand Studios

1

This combined restaurant, wine shop, and wine bar is integrated into the bottom floor of a small 1930s concrete industrial building near the entrance to the Bay Bridge. The architecture reflects this location through the use of plate steel, concrete, and rustic hardwood. The design of the new façade and foyer references the original sash windows of the building through the use of thin steel flat bar. The 12-foot-high front entrance door comprises irregularly angled glass panels, and its height gives the sense that a portion of the façade moves to allow access. The interior door from the foyer to the restaurant is more than 12 feet high and 8 inches deep. Although both doors are large and heavy, a sense of lightness is achieved through complementary use of thin edges of steel.

Lighting plays a key role in the composition of the interior. Textures of the concrete walls and the rough stone surfaces of the bars are emphasized with edge lighting. In the dining area those walls are screened with translucent fabric to soften sound and to add luminescence to the warehouse interior. Highlights of the interior also include suspended lighting elements specially designed and fabricated for the space. The interior of the wine shop comprises walls of suspended wine bottles. Delicate stainless steel ceiling-mounted cables hold fine metal rods and wood dowels to create a lacework of wine bottles floating off the rough concrete walls of the building. A continuous line of lighting on the edge of the floor emphasizes the texture of the industrial walls and backlights the suspended bottles giving a sense of depth and luminosity to this small enclosed space.

1 The dining area walls are screened with translucent fabric to soften sound and to add luminescence

2 Textures of the concrete and stone surfaces are emphasized with edge lighting

4

5

Opposite   Cables, metal rods, and wood dowels create a lacework of wine bottles

4 & 5   Interior highlights included suspended lighting elements specially
designed and fabricated for the space

Photography by Cesar Rubio

THE LOCAL VINE

SEATTLE, WASHINGTON, USA
Bohlin Cywinski Jackson

1

The Local Vine is a new wine bar in Seattle's vibrant Belltown neighborhood. Located in a prominent street-level space, the bar features tall ceilings and an abundance of natural light. The client asked the architects to create a prototypical design for a series of warm, accessible urban spaces where patrons could learn about and savor wine.

An inviting 17-foot-high wall of wine bottles directly opposite the main entry serves as a backdrop for wine tasters while providing an elegant storage solution. Overhead, an undulating Douglas fir ceiling draws patrons into the middle of the space and helps create intimate settings for conversation. The ceiling planes cleverly conceal an oversized mechanical unit that would have been costly to relocate or replace. A sleek, minimal fireplace opposite the bar has a raised hearth for casual seating, and glowing spherical lights softly illuminate the bar and fireplace, their playful shape easily visible to passersby outside.

The bar and built-in furnishings are custom designed using dark-stained plywood and blackened steel. Slotted plywood tables also designed by the architects complement a range of seating types from traditional bar and café to casual lounge seating. Wall colors chosen from a palette developed by the client range from bright red to deep burgundy and charcoal grey. Existing polished concrete floors were left exposed throughout. A small prep kitchen and new restrooms were added behind the bar. The Local Vine's clear delineation of spaces, modest palette of materials, and refined detailing offer a sophisticated setting for patrons to appreciate and enjoy fine wine.

1   The undulating Douglas fir ceiling draws patrons into the center of the bar
2   Glowing spherical lights illuminate the bar
3 & 4   The bar is a sophisticated setting for patrons of fine wine

Photography by Benjamin Benschneider

2

3

4

THE LOFT

LONDON, UK
Brinkworth

The concept for The Loft emulates a loft/warehouse conversion, with exposed raw materials and eclectic details making the bar an edgy yet comfortable, music-focused venue. Both client and design team were keen to retain the shell of the building—a first-floor unit with a concrete ceiling and a continuous, 14-foot-high expanse of window. Long curtains drop from a soffit down to a built-in drink shelf, enabling a complete cover of the windows if needed.

The impressive bar is the focal point of the venue and is constructed from Staffordshire Blue brick with a monolithic smooth cast and textured concrete top. The back bar fitting is slightly raised and framed by black block work, exposing the drink collection to maximum effect with its simplicity of design.

The acoustics became a fundamental issue driving the design, due to residents living above the venue. A suspended feature-ceiling raft, consisting of a series of inverse and converse pyramid-like shapes built in stained plywood, reflects and bounces the sound away from the concrete ceiling above. Chosen for their acoustical insulation properties, hollow bricks line the concrete walls, further enhancing the acoustics.

In the bar, seating is arranged into reservable areas with an eclectic mix of furniture that helps create a warehouse-like, laid-back atmosphere. The soft, comfortable leather seating, comprising both new and original pieces, balances out other harder finishes in the space. Each area feels self-contained without losing its place within the overall design scheme, and certain areas can be separated off or seating arrangements altered for various purposes.

1

1 White Eames chairs create contrast in the dining area

2 A suspended feature-ceiling raft reflects the sound away from the concrete ceiling above

2

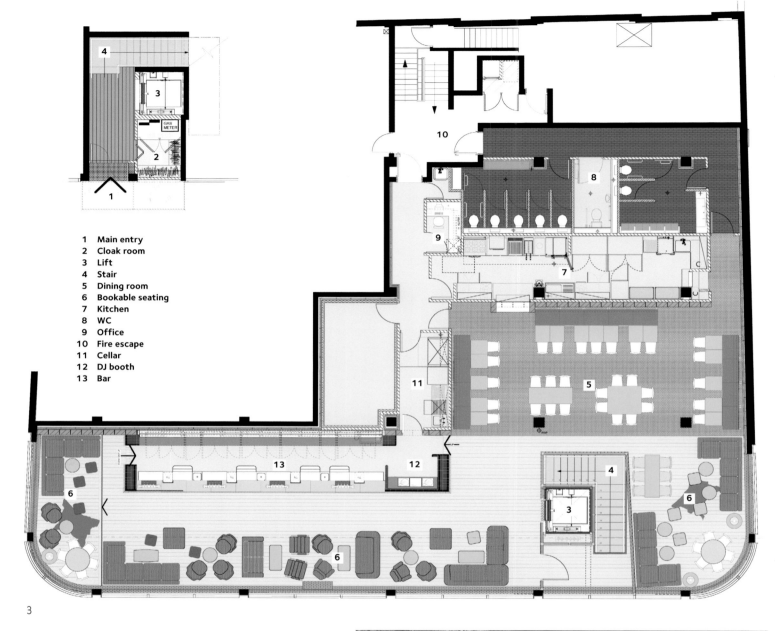

1 Main entry
2 Cloak room
3 Lift
4 Stair
5 Dining room
6 Bookable seating
7 Kitchen
8 WC
9 Office
10 Fire escape
11 Cellar
12 DJ booth
13 Bar

3

3 Floor plan

4 Chosen for their acoustical insulation properties, hollow bricks line the concrete walls

5 The back bar fitting is slightly raised, exposing the drink collection to maximum effect with its simplicity of design

6 The bar is constructed from Staffordshire Blue brick with a monolithic smooth cast and textured concrete top

7 A soft felt ceiling canopy wraps down two sides of the dining area

Photography by Alex Franklin

4

5

6

7

MINIBAR

1

minibar was created by three Dutch friends who had been looking for a different way of having a drink in the city. Fed up with queuing for drinks, trying to catch the bartender's eye, or being ignored at the bar, the trio came up with the idea of a bar offering private, well-stocked minibars in a relaxed, modern environment.

Housed in a former 1960s factory, the bar's façade has been restored using 13-foot-high, floor-to-ceiling wooden and glass panels set in a solid metal frame. To preserve this feeling of space and history, and also to keep the weather out when the doors are folded open, a glass façade was set back 5 feet inside the building. The small area created between the doors and the façade is a perfect space for smoking guests to connect with the street while still being undercover and part of the party.

To create a distinguished and luxurious atmosphere for the central area of Minibar, a variety of high-quality materials and furnishings were used. The custom-made stainless steel, leather, and oak furniture, in combination with warm colors, add contrast and style to the raw architectural base. The main area features three huge stainless steel fridges, each containing 15 color-coded minibars with their own number, lock, and transparent door. In keeping with the angular interior design, the fridges are placed at an 83-degree angle from the wall to allow people walking by a great view of, and into, the 45 minibars. The warm colors from the fridge complement the golden accents from the 18 suspended lamps, and the wooden floors and tables give this central area a warm atmosphere.

1 The bar is housed in a former 1960s factory

2 Floor plan

3 The glass façade is set back inside the building

4 The stainless steel, leather, and oak furniture is custom made

5 Three huge stainless steel fridges each contain 15 minibars

Photography by Ewout Huibers

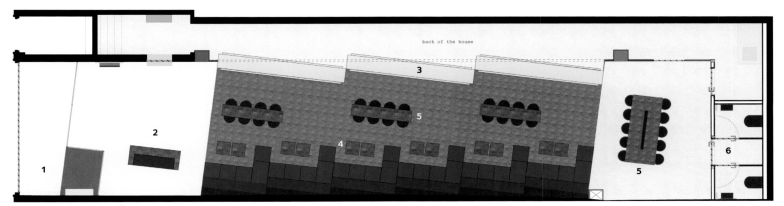

1 **Entry**
2 **Check-in desk**
3 **Fridges**
4 **Couches**
5 **Bar tables**
6 **Restrooms**

2

3

4

5

MINT NIGHTCLUB

PERTH, WESTERN AUSTRALIA, AUSTRALIA
Chindarsi Architects

Mint is an evening environment in which patrons can feel relaxed and comfortable without taking themselves too seriously. The concept behind the nightclub was born from an interest in suburbia, in particular, in the graphic and spatial potentials of suburban imagery and iconography. The not-so-subtle use of these helps to create a set of playful and irreverent spaces that take a tongue-in-cheek look at the places in which we live.

The use of domestic lighting, objects, and finishes that includes fence pickets, wall-hanging kookaburras, and garden gnomes lend the spaces a sense of familiarity and a finer scale. The reduction of certain pieces to white objects and their arrangement within the spaces is intended to challenge this familiarity, hopefully leading to a new or renewed appreciation of each.

1   Reception desk at the entry to the club

2   Nightclub elevation

3   Entry way from reception to the main floor area

4   Banquette seating in the main floor area

1

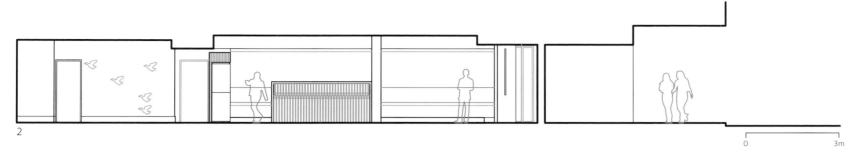

2

0   3m

3

4

6

7

5

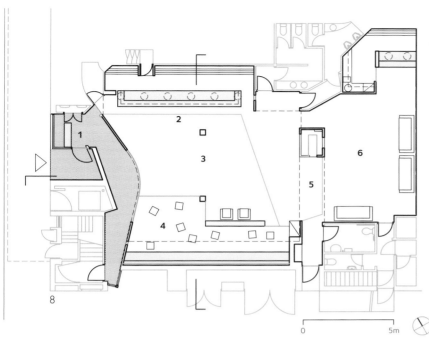

1 Entry
2 Bar
3 Main floor area
4 Raised lounge
5 DJ booth
6 Lounge bar

8

0   5m

5   Overall view from the main floor area
6   The lounge bar
7   Wall-hanging kookaburras
8   Floor plan
9   Seating and fence pickets in the main floor area
10 The bar in the main floor area

Photography by Emma van Dordrecht, F22 Photography

9

10

ꟿISHA ACAPULCO BAR LOUNGE

ACAPULCO, MEXICO
Pascal Arquitectos

This lounge bar in Acapulco is an entertainment venue dedicated to the senses. Color is used throughout the lounge to create an exciting visual experience. Access to the premises is by way of a wood-lined foyer that simulates the interior of a ship. Five high-definition screens are framed as oval windows that show either a cloudy sky traveling past at high speed or images from beneath the ocean.

A dark foyer leads to a wooden lounge decorated with small groups of sofas that look onto an outside smoking area. At one end of the lounge are several framed screens; on the other end is a 50-foot-long counter behind which sits a 10-foot-high by 50-foot-long high-definition video screen. Below the counter, geometric designs illuminated by LED lighting constantly change color.

The restrooms are exotic gathering places drenched in colored glass: the women's area is coordinated with red and white, with a bench and a huge palm tree at the center; the men's section is in black and blue, with a central triangular planter containing a tropical plant.

1   The wood-lined foyer
2   The entrance
3 & 4   The foyer leads to a lounge

1

2

3

4

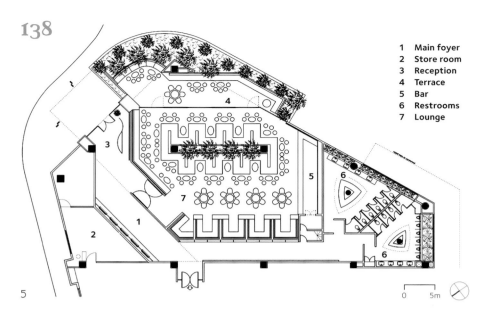

1 Main foyer
2 Store room
3 Reception
4 Terrace
5 Bar
6 Restrooms
7 Lounge

5 Floor plan

6 A view into the lounge

7 The 50-foot-long video screen dominates the lounge

8 Geometric designs are illuminated by LED lighting

9 Several framed screens are featured on one of the lounge walls

10 The women's restroom

Photography by Sófocles Hernández

0   5m

5

6

7

8

9

10

MISHA PALMAS

MEXICO CITY, MEXICO
Pascal Arquitectos

1

designed as an entertainment space for the over-30 crowd, the venue houses a lounge and a restaurant-bar connected by a lobby. The lobby, covered with black metal plates and dark terrazzo flooring, is illuminated by psychedelic images displayed on eight plasma screens. The lounge walls are completely covered in wood and surrounded by large windows that overlook a forest. Within this space are several small sets of living rooms, each with a plasma screen that recreates images such as a fireplace, a fish tank, or a landscape. The lush furniture is distributed around an exotic palm.

The restaurant-bar is surrounded by crystal walls that change color in combination with the music and the videos. This section also displays a 15-meter-long bar and further up, at the back, a 15-meter-long by 3-meter-high screen submerges the patrons into a virtual world—whether it be watching Earth from outer space, flying through the clouds, exploring a tropical forest, or swimming surrounded by sharks. The restrooms were designed as if they were part of the recreational spaces and are decorated with a service bar and a cozy sofa.

1   Bar

2   Lobby

2

3

Photography by Sófocles Hernández
  & Jaime Navarro

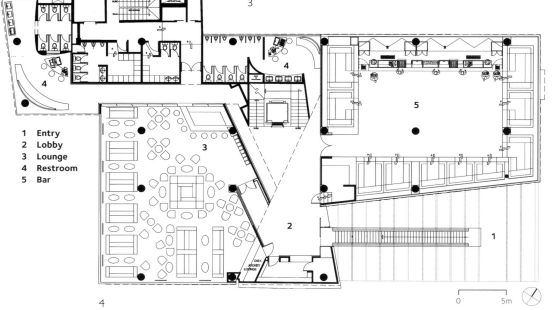

1   **Entry**
2   **Lobby**
3   **Lounge**
4   **Restroom**
5   **Bar**

4

0   5m

5

6

7

8

THE ONE BELOW

EDINBURGH, UK
TibbattsKirkAbel

1

The One Below is a unique, comfortable, and sophisticated late-night lounge that features the only "iBar" in the UK, an interactive, digital bar that produces stunning lighting effects. The bar also offers stylish private booths, complete with individual iPod docks and sunken champagne bucket tables. In developing the design of this unique bar, the owners traveled the world researching innovative bar concepts and the result is a stunning, uniquely designed late-night lounge.

The lounge's aesthetic is an amalgamation of ideas that the owner gave the interior designers and their interpretation of the concept of "raw materials." The brief was to create an original, contemporary late-night environment that incorporated the original Georgian features of the interior architecture. The creative uplighting system, which regularly changes color, enhances the original stone walls and key pieces of furniture. Other principal highlights include a 15-foot chaise longue covered with Italian-embossed Alma leather and entirely mirrored booths with central tables that change color. The choice of furniture also reflects the old and new: the lounge has an array of sumptuous Louis-style furniture with distinctly modern touches, allowing the lounge to be comfortable and contemporary at the same time.

1   Louis-style furniture in sumptuous purple
      against the stone walls

2   The interactive iBar

3

4

5

6

3   Drinks display behind the main bar changes color throughout
    the evening

4   The interactive iBar

5   Intimate velvet booth with built-in champagne bucket

6   Intimate iPod booths with sunken ice buckets

7   Floor plan

8   Flowers appear on the iBar when touched by a glass

Photography by Susie Lowe

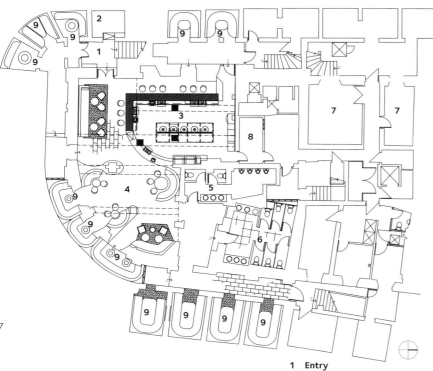

7

1   **Entry**
2   **Cloak room**
3   **Bar**
4   **Lounge**
5   **Men's restroom**
6   **Women's restroom**
7   **Cellar**
8   **Glass wash**
9   **Booth**

8

OSTERIA CICERI E TRIA

TORONTO, ONTARIO, CANADA
Giannone Petricone Associates

1   Entry vestibule

Opposite   Giro d'Italia mural

This 60-seat restaurant/bar reinterprets an age-old model of Italian hospitality—the *osteria*, or family-run tavern. The atmosphere is both intimate and sociable, with guests sharing tables and food. Old-world hospitality begins at the storefront entry, though once inside it is apparent that the rustic has been made modern; surfaces of reclaimed wood and stripped boards are routed with machined precision, inlayed with crisp steel, and punctuated with powder-coated industrial components.

The focal point is the communal table where 20 guests are encouraged to interact. At each place setting, the table edge has been inscribed with a traditional, Italian name. Rather than identifying patrons by table number, they are identified by this persona. With a slight adjustment of its spring-loaded lamp, the flour-covered pasta-making butcher block by day becomes the eight-person family dining table by night, still carved with a signature pasta recipe. The uniform distribution of crisply cut slots, pegs, and shelves allows the fully adaptable utility "peg wall" to be easily reconfigured for displays as needed.

Like the food, the architecture evokes quality and experiments with registering "the hand" that has fashioned it with an embedded layer of decorative and coded elements—such as family snapshots, a representation of the Giro d'Italia (Italy's famous Grand Tour road bicycle race), a mural mapping the major train stations of Italy, as well as doily patterns cured into the concrete. All elements of the design have been custom made, with the exception of the chairs, stools, and yellow industrial lights.

Photography by Ben Rahn

3

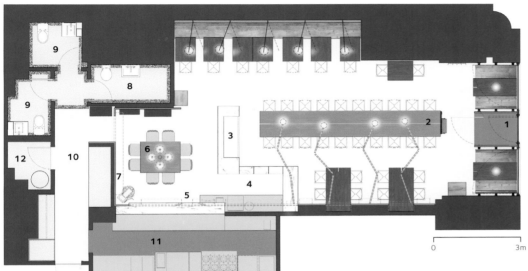

1   Vestibule
2   Communal table
3   Pasta fridge
4   Service bar
5   Pick up
6   Pasta-making table
7   Peg wall
8   Staff restroom
9   Restroom
10 Corridor
11 Kitchen
12 Utility room

0   3m

4

5

6

PADDINGTON INN

SYDNEY, NEW SOUTH WALES, AUSTRALIA
Indyk Architecture Pty Ltd

1

The Paddington Inn, located in a heritage-conservation area, has had a long history as a local inn. The main brief was to create a delightful courtyard for smokers that would also enliven the dark spaces of the rear of the hotel. The scooping out of the inner court, the "eye" of the building, gave the architects opportunity to develop a clear structural language of steel post-and-beam structure that supported the courtyard, the specialized acoustic panels, and the existing building. The rooms surrounding the courtyard are washed in daylight.

The interior planning upholds the various rooms of the old hotel. Most notably, the small nook with its Moorish-inspired stepped-timber ceiling, and the bistro/bar/lounge—a long room with its end focus being the bar and bronze-mirror reflections. The kitchen is faced with a wall of black-and-metallic glazed bricks and the ceiling of the bistro bar is a dance of moiré light and reflection.

The steel post-and-beam construction of the courtyard is refined and strong, bracing and supporting both the old and the new structure. The courtyard is an outdoor urban room, highly acoustically attenuated so that the patrons can enjoy it both day and night without the neighborhood being imposed upon. The stepped section of the courtyard allows for diversity of standing and seating areas. The mood changes between day and night have been carefully orchestrated to create mystery and delight. Through the courtyard one gets a glimpse of the wonderful front bar with its vibrant color scheme and reflective marble-mosaic wall. The structure and glazed walls of the courtyard extend to support a terrace on the first floor. This terrace is adjacent to a lounge and mobile bar.

2

3

4

1 Exterior view

2 Bistro bar lounge

3 The courtyard

4 View from bistro bar to courtyard

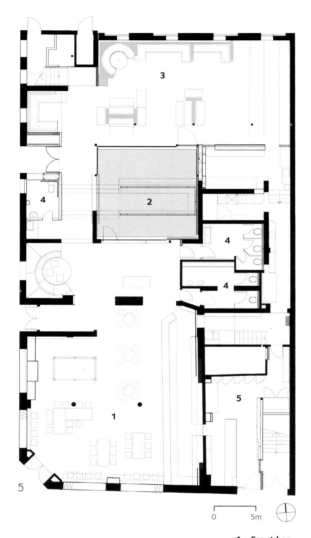

1 Front bar
2 Courtyard
3 Bistro bar
4 Restrooms
5 Bottleshop

6

7

8

9

10

Photography by Murray Fredericks

PLUNGE POOL BAR AT THE REGENT PALMS

PROVIDENCIALES, TURKS AND CAICOS ISLANDS
RAD Architecture and SWA Group

Plunge is located within The Regent Palms resort on the world-famous Grace Bay Beach. As the name suggests, Plunge is just as much poolside experience as an inside-the-pool experience. The bar comprises seating within the multi-million-dollar infinity-edge pool that allows guests to slide up to the bar without leaving the water, as well as four submerged bench-type seats that have their own table for the guests to rest their drinks. Sunken poolside dry seating is located between the pool, the bar, and main guest beach access, where guests can lounge at traditional bar stools or at a semicircular cushioned banquette and tables.

The Plunge Pool Bar was plunged in between the pools to allow for minimum interruption of views from the hotel units that are situated behind the bar. The area is serviced from a back-of-house service tunnel that runs throughout the resort property to keep service activities and guest interaction separate. The front side of the bar's dry seating area is clad with different shades of aqua-glass mosaic tiles to give guests the illusion of still being immersed in the pool.

1   Dry seating banquet detail
2   View of pool and bar from balcony
3   Plunge at night

1

2

3

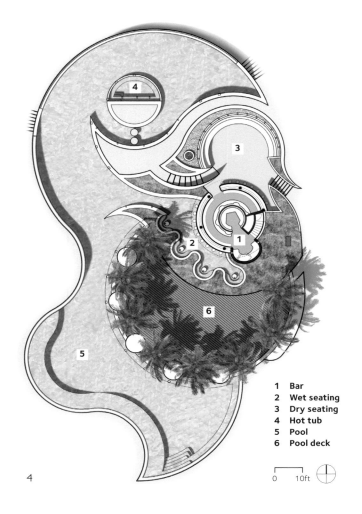

1 Bar
2 Wet seating
3 Dry seating
4 Hot tub
5 Pool
6 Pool deck

0   10ft

4

5

6

8

7

4   Pool plan

5   View of dry seating from pool deck

6   View of dry seating, bar, and wet seating

7   Pool elevation

8   View of bar from pool deck

**Photography courtesy of The Hartling Group
and RAD Architecture, Inc.**

POLO LOUNGE

SYDNEY, NEW SOUTH WALES, AUSTRALIA
Paul Kelly Design

1

The Oxford Hotel's basement and ground floor are targeted to the Sydney late night party market, while the Supper Club and the Polo Lounge on the top two levels are the ultimate VIP destination. The design was based on various concepts inspired from more than 200 bars and clubs from New York, Las Vegas, and Los Angeles. As patrons scale the glittering heights of the golden glow of the clear glass staircase that links both levels to the street, they become the ultimate VIP, entering a world of glamour, sophistication, and old world charm.

On Level One, the Supper Club is reminiscent of a SoHo New York bar with a focus on live performance. Raw exposed masonry walls are offset against vivid retro fabrics and playful ceiling moldings. On Level Two, at the zenith of the stair, is the Polo Lounge, the ultimate destination VIP bar. The space is timelessly elegant, reminiscent of a fabulous old-world Beverly Hills hotel. The light levels are low, the palette is kept to a bare minimum of chic black and white, and the walls are clad in highly ornate white gloss timber panels with black marble trims. A beautiful handmade rug sits on the oak parquetry floor and classic leather-buttoned Chesterfields are situated throughout the lounge. The views across the city are framed by the crystal-glass and leadlight trims of the balcony.

1   A clear glass staircase links both levels to the street
2 & 5   Polo Lounge
3   Supper Club bar
4   Restroom
6   Floor plan

Photography by Sharrin Rees

2

3

4

5

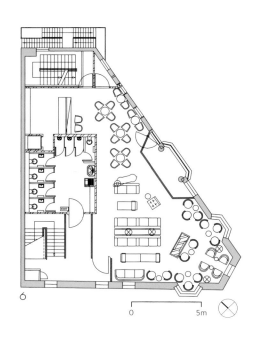

6

0   5m

POST OFFICE HOTEL

RICHMOND, VICTORIA, AUSTRALIA
Techne Architects

this bar was created within a compact and quirky Federation-style post office. The original building is sited on a peculiar triangular site and follows a style of design where spaces, windows, and door openings are all slightly non-symmetrical. The architects have designed a unique inner-city bar that takes advantage of the limited site and building areas, the engaging spaces, and details of the existing building. New building works included the construction of a kitchen that is literally squeezed between the post office and the railway overpass and the re-invention of an external courtyard space that fronts a main thoroughfare. This wedge-shaped courtyard is one of the most successful parts of the design; a one-time banal and semi-public space has been dramatically transformed with varied ground levels, built-in seats and tables, custom designed lighting, heating, and weather protection.

Inside, the marble and brass bar sits centrally with the activity of the kitchen visible behind and a new steel gantry constructed above for displaying and storing wine. Immediately in front of the bar is a standing area and beyond is a series of built-in tables and comfortable chairs on a podium level.

A surprise feature of the design came about when the ceiling in the entrance was removed to reveal the internal form and structure of the building's turret. By installing a chandelier and subtly detailing the form with mirrors, the architects were able to create an event space for the entry despite its small scale. Another feature of the design is the laser-cut steel graphic panels that have been incorporated into the design throughout. Created by artist Clare McCracken, the design weaves the abstracted bird's-wing graphic through architectural elements, signage, and branding.

1   The wedge-shaped courtyard

Opposite   Exterior view of the Post Office Hotel

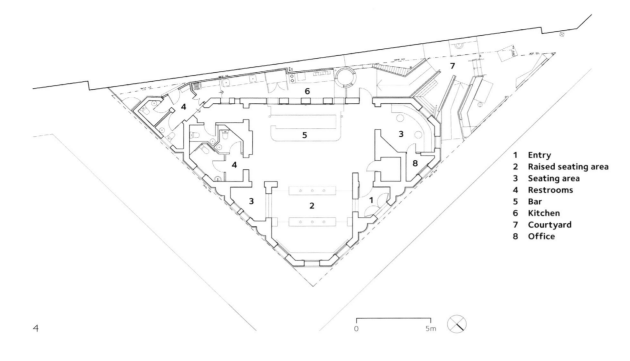

4

1 Entry
2 Raised seating area
3 Seating area
4 Restrooms
5 Bar
6 Kitchen
7 Courtyard
8 Office

0   5m

Opposite & 6   The marble and brass bar

4   Floor plan

5   View of inside of the turret

7 & 8   Laser-cut steel panels incorporate the abstracted bird's-wing graphic throughout

Photography by Matt Kennedy

5

6

7

8

Q-BAR
VALLETTA WATERFRONT, MALTA
Architecture Project (AP)

1

inspired by the mid 18th-century Baroque Vaults at Pinto Stores on the Valletta Waterfront, the concept for Q-bar's interior structure is based on the stacking of wooden crates to form sculptural, tower-like volumes. By night, the timber batten-clad structures are illuminated, and combined with the inner layer of multicolored tiles and the floor pattern of intersecting lines, the design achieves a cityscape-like visual effect.

The wooden structures serve to modulate the volume within the interior and also house its essential services. The composition of the timber volumes guide the visitor through the space, while the programmed lighting engages with these structures, creating intriguing changes in their mass and overall ambience of the venue. The interior areas within the bar are undefined and open to interpretation, with the dominating timber structure and textures dictating the interior spaces. For example, the upper seating area is seen as an extension of the main bar, which is located beneath it, while the DJ area is a specific function housed within a timber crate-like structure. Throughout the space, the play on color and texture allows the visitor to follow the workings of the interior rather than the conventional layout of a bar with its traditional eating area, chill-out lounge, or disc jockey stand.

1 Night view showing back lighting of the bar

2 Night view of main bar back-lit with blue lights

3 View of main bar and upper seating area, showing floor design with purple back lighting of the bar

4 View of main bar with seating area above and DJ area at the far back, with details of floor design and pink lights

5 View of DJ and restroom areas

6 Restroom tiles and sink detail

Photography by Alberto Favaro

2

4

3

5

6

THE REFINERY

LONDON, UK
Fusion Design & Architecture Ltd

Located in the landmark Blue Fin Building, this bar's sophisticated, industrial-themed design is softened by touches of color and texture throughout. Floor-to-ceiling glass walls invite guests into the main space and a host of flexible, eclectically styled smaller areas. The refinery has been cleverly designed with different spaces such as a mezzanine-level private dining room, classic dining and refectory style tables, and curtained circular booths alongside high drinking tables and bar stools. Soft, tan leather slung chairs and tables sit within olive green and jet black retro lighting. A wine wall provides a striking design element above the bar and complements the Enomatic system built-in below.

The refinery takes its love of wine seriously, offering more than 50 bins including over 40 of their best vintages by the glass. A unique swipe-card system allows guests to top up their card and purchase wine directly from a specially designed point-of-sale system, eliminating the need to queue at the bar. The refinery's spacious interior can cater private events, launches, and parties for small groups or larger gatherings of up to 550 guests, including 236 seated. The private dining area, perched on the mezzanine level, allows up to 12 guests to dine in exclusive style while looking down on the decadence below. A stunning al fresco terrace, complete with bright-orange seating and black and white parasols, provides a further 120 covers in warmer months.

1   The wine wall above the bar provides a striking design element
2   Floor-to-ceiling glass walls invite guests inside

1

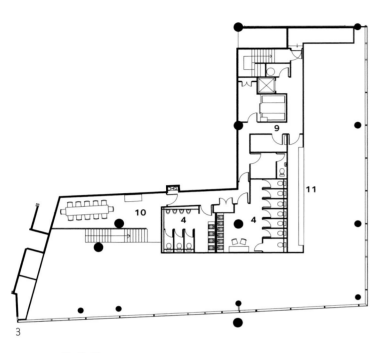

3

3   Mezzanine floor plan

4   Ground floor plan

5–7 The refinery has been cleverly designed with areas such as a mezzanine-level private dining room, classic dining and refactory style tables alongside high drinking tables and bar stools

Photography by Media Wisdom

5

1   **Bar/lounge area**
2   **Bar/tall-seating area**
3   **Dining area**
4   **Restroom**
5   **Preparation area**
6   **Food servery**
7   **Cellar**
8   **Bar servery**
9   **Storeroom**
10 **Private dining area**
11 **Wine wall**

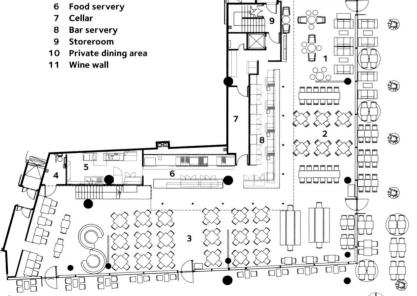

4

6

7

ROCKPOOL BAR AND GRILL

SYDNEY, NEW SOUTH WALES, AUSTRALIA
Bates Smart

1

The Art Deco City Mutual Building in Sydney contains a 1936 banking chamber of magnificent proportions and drama. The new Rockpool Bar and Grill has been installed into this space, in which soaring, 40-foot-high columns frame the main dining space while adjacent spaces contain more intimate dining areas and an open kitchen.

The bar space opens directly off the street and glimpses of the venue can be caught through the tinted doors of the wine glass chandeliers, which provide a soft glow and sparkle to the bar area. The bar comprises a series of small intimate spaces with a mood reminiscent of speakeasy establishments. The walls and ceilings are finished in a patterned wallpaper, which adds a level of richness and further underscores the design and era of the original building. The bar's lighting levels are low, with focused highlights and warm washes further enhancing the refined ambience.

Sydney venues are often centered around the view and the drama of the harbor; in contrast, this space offers an embracing and elegant dining room where delight in food, wine, and conversation is the focus. According to the architect, one of the primary goals for this venue was to celebrate the remarkable volume of the space and its dramatic qualities. A core challenge was to insert enough into the space for patrons to feel they are among the selected few but still ensure they are able to experience the room in its entirety.

1   Entry is via grand Art Deco doors

2   Custom furnishings create intimate spaces throughout

3

4

5

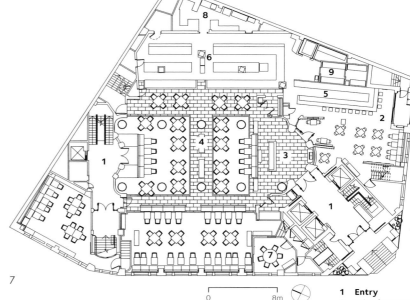

7

1 Entry
2 Wine bar entry
3 Reception
4 Restaurant
5 Bar
6 Open kitchen
7 Private dining
8 Wash up
9 Cellar

3 & 5 The magnificent central space has a 40-foot ceiling

4 The bar is designed as an informal yet sophisticated space

6 A table with a view

7 Floor plan

8 The bar offers an elegant yet relaxed setting for 45 people

Photography by Earl Carter

8

THE RUM DIARIES

SYDNEY, NEW SOUTH WALES, AUSTRALIA
Re:love

Set behind a brick-arched frontage, The Rum Diaries is a great visual restaurant. Walking inside, patrons are immediately exposed to a comfortable mix of worn yet inviting colonial grandeur. This is complemented by an eclectic collection of ornaments and furniture, ranging from the high era of Art Deco to the assured hip retro of the early 1960s Danish sofa—and creates an inviting, lived-in atmosphere.

There are three rooms to dine in, each with a different feel. The front room, paneled with burnished dark wood, features a cocktail bar built from recycled railway sleepers. The second room, a candle-lit space, allows a good view into the kitchen where diners can see the chefs hard at work, and where a small bell announces the emergence of each fresh dish. At the back, past the exquisite Deco tiled bathroom, is the "secret room"—available at the invitation of staff only. The Oscar Acosta Room (named after the legendary Chicano lawyer, and real life Dr Gonzo attorney from Hunter S. Thompson's *Fear and Loathing in Las Vegas*) is a funky, comfortable area for kicking back with more cocktails post-eating amid the ambience created by the exposed brickwork, white Queen Anne fireplace, and an old wall-length bookcase hiding secret doors.

1 The brick-arched frontage

2–5 The cocktail bar

2

3

4

5

6 & 8   An eclectic collection of ornaments and furniture

7   Rum-inspired cocktails

9   The Oscar Acosta Room

10 & 11   A comfortable mix of worn yet inviting colonial grandeur

Photography by Sabine Albers

7

8

6

9

10

11

SASHI SUSHI + SAKE LOUNGE

MANHATTAN BEACH, CALIFORNIA, USA
KAA Design Group

1

Combining the best in Japanese cuisine and modern design, Sashi Sushi + Sake Lounge raises the bar for the South Bay culinary scene. Inspired by the beachside locale and delectable menu developed by celebrity chef Makoto Okuwa, the design team utilized a variety of exotic materials and a warm color palette to create a sophisticated space with an air of well-appointed modernism.

For the bar and lounge area, the designers incorporated horizontal slats of bubinga wood stacked from floor to ceiling to comprise the walls, which reveal internally lit niche openings to the dining area. Above, the ceiling is a flood of twinkling lights, which heightens the interplay of warm woods and colorful accents that brighten the space. The sake bar adds an additional splash of color, with its internally illuminated magenta glass back and steel façade. In the lounge, custom wood-framed settees with plum-colored cushions and orange- and magenta-toned pillows are visually captivating, relaxing, and inviting.

1   The custom wood-framed settees in the sake lounge
2   Floor plan
3   The sake bar's internally illuminated magenta glass backing
4   The exterior sake bottle display

Photography by Karyn Millet

1   Exterior entry lounge
2   Entry lounge
3   Lounge
4   Outdoor dining terrace
5   Sake bar
6   Sake back bar
7   Main dining room
8   Sushi bar
9   Sushi kitchen
10 Front kitchen
11 Dishwashing area
12 Back kitchen
13 Restroom
14 Trash
15 Office

SCARPETTA

NEW YORK, NEW YORK, USA
S. Russell Groves

Scott Conant, well-known chef of L'Impero and Alto fame, worked closely with the architect to design this venue, located on the edge of Manhattan's meatpacking district. The space perfectly reflects Conant's vision of "Urban Milan meets Tuscany" and the theme of "old versus new" also echoes throughout the design. The first of two distinct areas, the front café houses casual seating for 20 and features a long, turn-of-the-century bar. Stained a deep black and topped by slick Carrera marble, it takes on a contemporary edge, punctuated by sparkling mercury glass fixtures. In addition, panels of tawny beechwood veneer, sandwiched between glass and blackened steel, act as unique dividers.

The main dining room features a retractable roof, offset by rough-hewn timber beams. Lining the walls is pickled white cork cut in a random grid pattern, which complements long, ochre-colored banquettes and period-inspired sconces. In a touch of whimsy, mirrors hung by rusty brown belted straps add an industrial note and pop of color. The space is at once warm, inviting, and casual, but also sleek and sophisticated.

1   Main dining area with retractable skylight

Opposite   Rusty brown leather banquette with oak trim

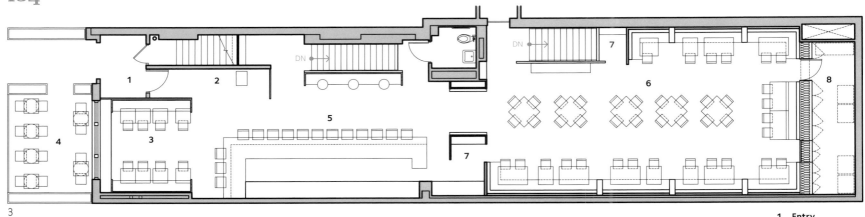

3

1 Entry
2 Reception
3 Café
4 Outdoor dining
5 Bar
6 Main dining
7 Service station
8 Wine cooler

4

5

6

7

3   Floor plan

4   Bar area with café beyond

5   Ebonized oak bar and polished Calacatta gold marble floor

6   Café featuring glass box chandelier framed in dark bronze

7   Bathroom with custom mirrors hung by rusty brown leather straps
    with polished nickel buckles

Photography courtesy of S. Russell Groves

SECOND HOME KITCHEN AND BAR

DENVER, COLORADO, USA
Andre Kikoski Architect

The design of this Colorado bar and restaurant is warm and welcoming, inspired by the character of the surrounding Rocky Mountains. This 5,000-square-foot space comprises a series of areas characterized by a calm, residential-like quality.

The interior materials underpin the authenticity of the venue as a part of the Rocky Mountain environment. Rich textures such as pony-skin and wood-paneled walls, bark tile, and reclaimed wood contrast with stone, stainless steel, and glass to create an intriguing and thoughtful material palette. The sober geometry of the plan is complemented by unembellished drystack stone walls and rough, wood-plank ceilings. Design elements such as graffiti-printed upholstery on Arne Jacobsen Egg Chairs and artisan-quality 1950s Italian chandeliers accent the space, bringing a stroke of whimsy and animation. All materials were locally sourced and local craftsmen played an integral role in the execution of the design.

The design effortlessly knits together the comforts and joys of a mountain vacation home with the modern aesthetics and wit of a sophisticated venue. The space envelops patrons in comfortable surrounds and juxtaposes the austere and theatrical with architecture that grounds the bar and restaurant in its Colorado setting.

1   The private dining room
2   The bar with outdoor seating beyond

2

3   The main dining room

4   Floor plan

5   The wine storage and seating area through
    the forest-salvaged butternut glass panels

6   Detail view of outdoor seating area

7   Bar seating

8   Bar looking back to the lounge

9   Detail view of private dining room

Photography by Eric Laignel

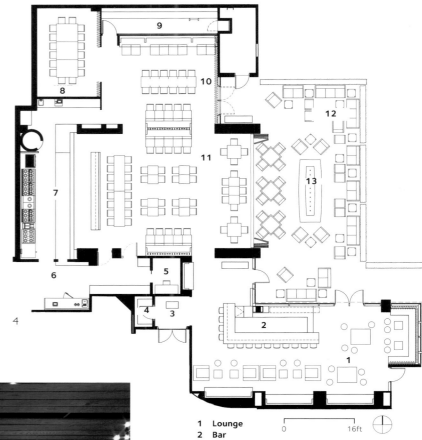

4

1   **Lounge**
2   **Bar**
3   **Vestibule**
4   **Coatroom**
5   **Manager's office**
6   **Kitchen**
7   **Kitchen/servery**
8   **Private dining**
9   **Wine adega**
10 **Semi-private dining**
11 **Main dining**
12 **Outdoor seating**
13 **Firepit**

3

5

6

7

8

9

SKYBAR AT TRADERS HOTEL

KUALA LUMPUR, MALAYSIA
Traders Hotel Kuala Lumpur

1

Located on level 33 of the hotel, this area is a pool facility during the day while at night it becomes a bar with fabulous views of the city's skyline, particularly the spectacular Petronas Twin Towers. In fact, it's said that the view at night is "worth a million smiles!" The idea for the bar was conceptualized during the construction of the hotel after it was realized that it would be a shame to let this space go to waste in the evenings when the pool facility closed.

The bar is designed to be a comfortable place to chill, while maintaining a hip, contemporary, and stylish feel. Lighting in the bar is an important part of the overall design as it helps to complement both the illumination of the Twin Towers and the view of the city's skyline at night. A glass roof covers most of the bar, but is left open above the pool; retractable blinds can be pulled down to provide protection from the rain. Cabanas have been incorporated into what were once just empty crevices, and these have turned out to be the bar's most popular seating areas.

1 SkyBar from a bird's-eye view featuring the Petronas Twin Towers shimmering in the distance
2 SkyBar sign
3 A pool by day becomes a bar at night
4 Cocktails to go with the views that are "worth a million smiles!"
5 At all angles the Petronas Twin Towers are a prominent feature of the view
6 The cabanas along the windows are popular seating areas

Photography courtesy of SkyBar, Traders Hotel Kuala Lumpur

2

3

4

5

6

Sleek

EDG Interior Architecture + Design

1

To complement his new steakhouse concept in St. Louis, Chef Hubert Keller was inspired by the idea of creating an ultra-lounge in the contemporary Lumière Place Casino to provide a hip, late-night venue and treat both locals and visitors to a high-energy urban experience in the heart of steak country.

The design concept evolved from research into the history of St. Louis as the termination point of the traditional Texas cattle drives. The interior is influenced by the imagery associated with prime beef shipped eastward on the first refrigerated boxcars, with their thick slabs of ice in roofs and walls. This story of range and pasture, boxcars, rails, and ice became the inspiration for the contemporary approach to materials used throughout the design.

Angled vistas and horizontal wood walls were enlivened with "ice-like" lanterns, while walls of warm marble recall the organic quality of cattle drive maps. The ultra-lounge was fitted with a stretched "boxcar" lounge, and the back bar was fashioned as a series of glowing slabs of ice, supporting the metaphor for movement. Inspired by the weathered wood of boxcars, railway ties, and pasture fences, the design makes significant use of re-sawn timber as a wall treatment, incorporating more than five species of reclaimed wood to create a varied texture throughout the restaurant.

2

1 & 2   The first refrigerated boxcars used to ship prime beef from St Louis
were the inspiration behind the design

3

4

3 The back bar is fashioned as a series of glowing slabs of ice

4 Private dining room

5 Temperature-controlled wine room

6 Floor plan

7 & 8 The design makes significant use of re-sawn timbers and marble as a wall treatment to create a varied texture throughout the restaurant

Photography by Eric Laignel

5

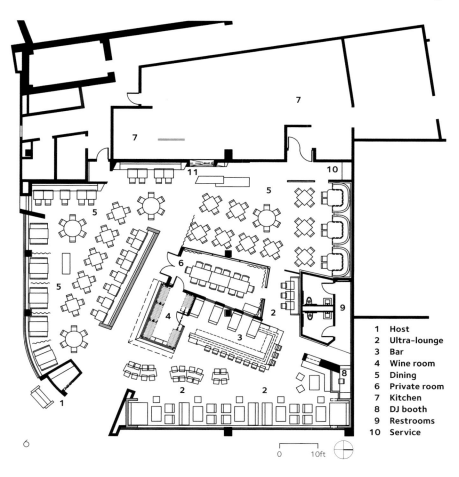

6

1 Host
2 Ultra-lounge
3 Bar
4 Wine room
5 Dining
6 Private room
7 Kitchen
8 DJ booth
9 Restrooms
10 Service

0   10ft

7

8

SPICE TEMPLE

SYDNEY, NEW SOUTH WALES, AUSTRALIA
Bates Smart

1

Located on the basement level of a magnificent 1936 Art Deco building, which also houses the Rockpool Bar and Grill, the entry door to Spice Temple is a large plasma screen offering alluring images of Chinese fabric gently moving in the wind, which then reveals a delicately carved timber door. The journey down the curved stairs gradually introduces a softly lit space where raw painted brickwork walls, exposed structure, and cement sheet floor are all neutrally colored to form the bar space. The patterned glass openings at the end of the bar allow glimpses of the activity in the kitchen beyond. The bar, framed with shadowy lighting and mesh, offers guests a unique selection of cocktails that draw inspiration from the 12 signs of the Chinese zodiac.

Materiality is basic, for example a hanging timber screen that divides the bar from the dining area made from sawn timber planks dipped in red paint. The mood in the bar is raw and lively, in contrast to the dining area where the finishes are softer, the lighting subdued and focused, and where acoustics are calm and colors warm. While there is little reference to Asia in the architecture, Spice Temple's design has been influenced by the street hawker food markets and links to a menu that draws inspiration from the provinces of Sichuan, Yunnan, Hunan, Jiangxi, Guangxi, and Xinjiang.

The venue's spaces have been made intimate and the seating is dense to enhance the atmosphere and relax the mood. The temperature setting is intentionally higher than normal and vivid color throughout Spice Temple adds to the sense of vibrancy. The dramatic, theatrical lighting and screening devices create a sense of personal space and privacy in this relatively small venue. Commissioned photographic portraits by Earl Carter of striking Asian women add mystery and intrigue.

2

3

1   A hanging timber screen divides the bar from the dining area

2   The dining area

3   The lighting throughout is subdued and focused

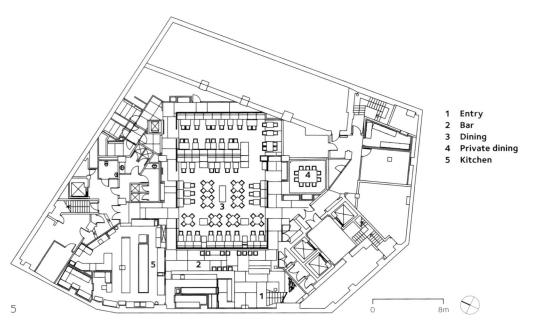

1 Entry
2 Bar
3 Dining
4 Private dining
5 Kitchen

4   The bar

5   Floor plan

6 & 7   Theatrical lighting and screening devices create
       a sense of privacy

8   Photographic portraits by Earl Carter add mystery
     and intrigue

**Photography by Earl Carter (1–3,6,8)
   and Marcus Clinton (4,7)**

5

0   8m

4

6

7

8

STREET

LOS ANGELES, CALIFORNIA, USA
Neil M. Denari Architects Inc.

STREET is celebrity chef Susan Feniger's first solo restaurant, offering a pan-cultural menu of street inspired tastes. Located in the heart of Hollywood, this project consists of an interior space with mezzanine and an exterior dining patio. The design merges the colors and material tactility of the urban street into a coherent atmospheric world that avoids thematic associations in favor of more abstract techniques.

The interior envelope of the main dining room is a dark-stained wood surface that encompasses both wall and ceiling, splitting in parallel fashion to allow for large areas of graphic art by the London-based artists Huntley-Muir. Bright reds and oranges punctuate this world, making reference, though not literally, to the signage systems found in cities. Here, the relationship between the flatness of the 2D world is brought into a state of high contrast against the deep 3D space of the wood surface. As an accumulated whole, the space collects together the worlds of art, advertising, vernacular materials, and abstract geometry in the attempt to project a sense of warmth within a globalized, omni-cultural dining experience.

1   Exterior view
2   Front view looking toward interior dining space and mezzanine
Opposite   Rear view looking toward bar and front entrance

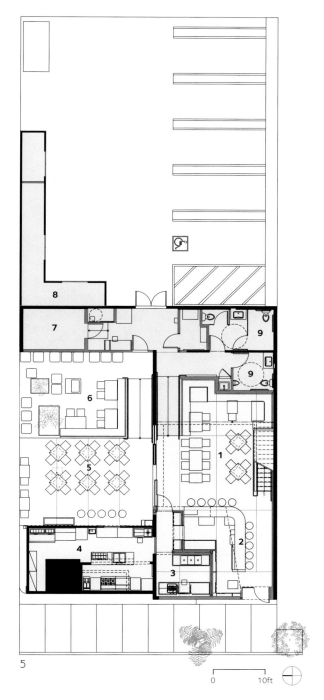

5

6

1 Dining area
2 Bar
3 Dishroom
4 Kitchen
5 Lower patio
6 Upper patio
7 Refrigerator
8 Store room
9 Restrooms

Opposite From mezzanine looking down at bar with ceiling view

5 Floor plan

6 Mezzanine ceiling view

Photography courtesy of NMDA, Inc

SUGARCANE

LAS VEGAS, NEVADA, USA
ICRAVE

Sugarcane, the boutique nightclub concept of Sushi Samba, is separated from the restaurant by a long corridor that acts as a transitional element between the two distinct spaces and offers guests respite from the high-energy, carnival-inspired restaurant. At the end of the corridor, Sugarcane, a Favela-inspired late-night space, has a muted palette that creates a sultry atmosphere and pays homage to the iconography of Sugarcane's key DNA. A stage, dance floor, and DJ booth are highlighted by materials that have a raw, natural feel—including gold and chocolate brown leather, bamboo, rustic wood, smoked and frosted acrylic, resin, and paper.

A custom-designed sugarcane-inspired ceiling is a combined architectural and lighting element. Moving lights wind through tubes and rods that begin as a ceiling element and transform into performance poles. The VIP area is styled to include plush seating, mood lighting, third-world relics, and Brazilian Favela found objects. The public space of the club flows to the restrooms, creating vistas into and out of the rooms, playing with the concept of privacy as a performance space. Bathroom pods are scaled to recall oversized sugarcane and are colored with graffiti by Brazilian artist Felipe "Flip" Yung.

1   Entrance to Sugarcane from Sushi Samba

2   A long corridor separates Sushi Samba from Sugarcane

3   Custom graffiti by Brazilian graffiti artist Felipe "Flip" Yung

2

3

4

5

6

4   Main bar

5   View of the stage, dance floor, and DJ booth

6   View of VIP room from the bar

7   Sugarcane-inspired tubular DJ booth

Photography by Francis + Francis

7

THE SUGARMILL

SYDNEY, NEW SOUTH WALES, AUSTRALIA
David Hicks Pty Ltd

The Sugarmill is a new concept in Sydney. It takes the flavor of Melbourne's The George Wine Room in St Kilda and adds a touch of New York's Pastis, frequented by the girls on *Sex in the City*. The theme is quirky, relaxed, tactile and earthy.

Mixing concepts of urban glamour and eclectic styles has resulted in a sophisticated, warm and very bespoke design. The palette consists of vintage ochre wall tiling, raw travertine flooring bordered by antique Argentinian black-and-white marble trims sourced from Buenos Aires. Specialist paint features set off grand coffered ceilings complete with pressed-metal inserts and intricate plasterwork cornicing. Italian-style dark-stained timber and a beveled mirror are features of the bar. The front of the bar is made from Macassar timber with detailed timber moldings.

1   The outdoor drinking area is always popular on a fine day

2 & 4   Custom-designed bottle display with timber and mirror

3   Ground floor plan

Following pages
   Main bar seating area with feature bar pendants in the background

Photography by Shannon McGrath

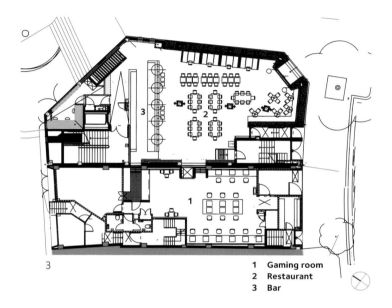

3

1 Gaming room
2 Restaurant
3 Bar

2

4

tHE SWAN BAR AT THE GLOBE

LONDON, UK
Brinkworth

this renovation of the restaurant and bar within Shakespeare's infamous Globe Theatre on the South Bank of the Thames is a contemporary venue that retains a strong sense of the site's history. Multiple mild steel-based tables are placed throughout the bar, differing only in their surface tops of burnt oak, natural oak, and zinc. The interior design features three large sharing tables running the center of the room, reminiscent of a domestic kitchen environment. These tables are overhung by an idiosyncratic lighting feature comprising 50 bare, round light bulbs of varying dimensions hung at different heights from an Anaglypta ceiling panel, interspersed with The Swan's signature, Ingo Maurer–designed, winged light bulbs.

Enhancing the relaxed atmosphere of a domestic environment, vintage furniture has been used to create an informal lounge area. The area is further defined by the use of a variety of flooring materials. In the more relaxed lounge, long, narrow stone tiles gradually bleed into timber floorboards of similar dimensions in the dining area. The main bar is made from marble and is multifunctional, allowing for both food preparation and drinks service.

1   Vintage stainless steel lamps are hung along the length of the space
2   Timber floorboards gradually bleed into the stone tiles

4

5

6

7

1 Entry
2 Terrace
3 Cashier
4 Kitchen
5 Bar
6 Food servery
7 Seating area

3   The light feature in the ceiling comprises 50 bare light bulbs of varying dimensions

4   Vintage furniture in a lounge area to the rear of the bar

5   The use of natural materials creates a warm and subtle color palette

6   The marble bar is multifunctional, allowing for food preparation and drinks service

7   Floor plan

Photography by Louise Melchior

t-012

Ippolito Fleitz Gorup + i_d buero

1

t-012 was designed as an homage to Germany's first president, Theodor Heuss, who is remembered not only for his political achievements but also as a *bon viveur* with a fine sense of humor, famous for his quotations dedicated to the more pleasurable side of life. A distinctive black-and-white, urban visual theme was developed for the interior design of this three-level bar.

As the entrance is somewhat hidden beneath the arcades of the building, a horizontal lighting element made of large Perspex boxes was installed as street signage. Inside, the main bar space welcomes the guest with a freestanding, U-shaped bar made of white Corian and a backdrop of black-stained, brushed wood with large white painted illustrations. The illustrations are surreal adaptations of urban themes, juxtaposed with street-life objects such as a real streetlamp. The ceiling is covered with hexagonal mirrors, giving extra height to the space.

The back area of the ground floor comprises two smaller lounge areas. The first is a polygonal room with mirrored walls; reflections from the mirrors in combination with a ceiling dotted with LED lamps make the space appear never-ending. The second lounge provides the perfect counterfoil: a black, leather-clad space that enfolds a white, illuminated table beneath a mirrored ceiling. On the upper floor, which feaures a large dance floor, a large ceiling illustration receives the guests and visually draws them toward the bar, where bottles set on chrome steps create a broad and inviting backdrop. The basement level houses another smaller dance floor and bar, as well as the cloakroom and toilets. Wall and ceiling motifs display images of insects and carnivorous plants, while the staircase serves as a connective element and features hedonistic quotations from Theodor Heuss.

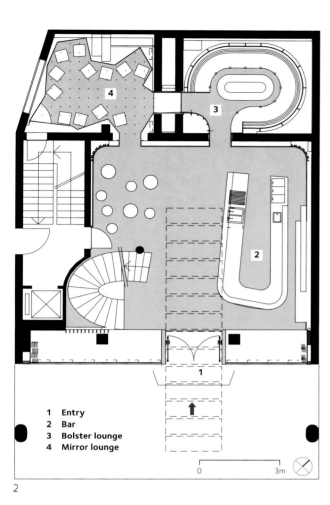

2

1 Entry
2 Bar
3 Bolster lounge
4 Mirror lounge

0   3m

1   U-shaped bar

2   Floor plan

3 & 5   Illustrations of urban themes are juxtaposed with street-life objects

4 & 6   Mirrored walls and a ceiling dotted with lamps make the space appear never-ending

Photography by Zooey Braun

3

4

5

6

TIPPLING CLUB

DEMPSEY HILL, SINGAPORE
Matthew Bax, Ryan Clift, and Jerry de Souza

Tucked away in the lush landscape of Singapore's Dempsey Hill and housed in former British colonial army barracks, Tippling Club is a bar and restaurant acclaimed for its brilliant pairing of avant-garde cocktails and modern cuisine. With this striking venue, co-owners head-bartender Matthew Bax, who designed the bottle display and bar stations, and head-chef Ryan Clift, who designed the kitchens, are elevating the status of the handcrafted cocktail and challenging the rules of fine dining.

Inspired by the *Wrapped Reichstag* in Berlin by artists Christo and Jeanne-Claude, designer Jerry de Souza has created an equally progressive yet relaxed setting for guests. The goal was to marry the colonial past of the existing building with a modern skin and the surrounding jungle. Preserving the historical significance of the building, a modern annex was added to the original structure using a mix of canvas, recycled industrial rubber, stainless steel, glass, and wood. A clear membrane on the internal wall provides patrons with an uninterrupted view of the forest. This allows the building to "breathe" while serving a functional purpose as a transparent barrier against the elements.

A chic industrial bar gives both diners and drinkers front-row seats to the action at the bar and kitchen. Overhead, an elaborate bottle installation of rare spirits hangs within reach of the bartenders—a design element that was created as a tribute to Bax's Melbourne bar, Der Raum. Outside, a newly constructed open-air forest terrace allows guests to enjoy cocktails under a canopy of trees and stars.

2

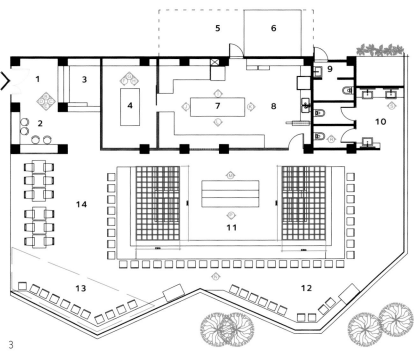

3

4

5

1 Entry
2 Waiting area
3 Reception
4 Test kitchen
5 Shelter
6 Cold room
7 Kitchen
8 Washing
9 Staff restroom
10 Restrooms
11 Bar
12 Chill-out area
13 Smoking area
14 Dining

1 Bar view of the "spice rack": a wide range of spices, food chemicals, and flavors used in the food and cocktails

2 Counter seating is shared by drinkers and diners

3 Floor plan

4 Alternative back bar seating overlooking the forest

5 Tools of the trade hanging above the bar station

Photography by Stephen Black

*t*WOTWENTYTWO AT THE LANDMARK LONDON

LONDON, UK
Fusion by Design

1

Part of the prestigious, five-star The Landmark London hotel in Marylebone, twotwentytwo is the result of a recent renovation and fit out by a leading UK design firm. Sympathetically refurbished, this restaurant and bar combines traditional elements with eclectic modern features. The original oak-wood paneling, sculpted ceilings, and antique fireplaces from the Grade II listed building have been retained, while the bespoke furniture is upholstered in glossy leathers and fabrics by Zoffany, Andrew Martin, and Harlequin Harris.

Custom-made banquette seating provides a focal point in the main space, and bespoke pendants are suspended over butcher-block-style tables that feature polished pewter tops with inset champagne bowls. As a playful reference to the horse-drawn carriages that used to deliver guests to The Landmark London's courtyard, a life-sized black horse lamp by Moooi has been positioned at the entrance. Elegant lighting is key to the design, and three contemporary "Flower of Life" chandeliers by Willowlamp, which were hand-made in South Africa, glisten through hundreds of silver beads. Additional features include a 36-foot-long Chesterfield-style sofa, polished oversized mirrors, a wine library, and two specially commissioned artworks set next to the original fireplace.

1   External signage
2   Overall view

3

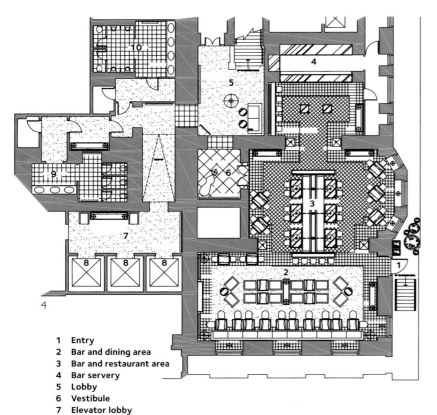

4

1 Entry
2 Bar and dining area
3 Bar and restaurant area
4 Bar servery
5 Lobby
6 Vestibule
7 Elevator lobby
8 Elevators
9 Women's restroom
10 Men's restroom

5

3   Seating area view

4   Floor plan

5   Central poseur and
    banquette view

**Photography by Faye Hatton
Photography**

ᴜᴦRBAN REEF

BOSCOMBE BAY, UK
Macaulay Sinclair

1

ᴜᴦban Reef is a unique combination of a bar, decked external terrace with a restaurant, café, and deli outlet that functions as a vibrant social hub. Taking the building's architecture as the starting point, the designers used eye-catching visual references and color palettes from the 1950s, including furniture, materials, and finishes that were influenced by transport posters, advertisements, and seaside resort branding. As a result, on the ground floor the colors are energetic and snappy, while the design forms are simple, efficient, and functional referencing the simplicity and functionality of post-war furniture. The designers also referenced post-war Britain's renewed relationship with the seaside by using beach huts and weatherboarding.

The oversized bar and kitchen ensures that the 80-seat external decking can be efficiently served during peak summer months. Also incorporated into the design is a linear space across the front of the ground floor with excellent physical and visual cues with the deck and beyond via three sets of double-glazed doors.

On the first floor a mezzanine accommodates an additional 40 patrons and a second stairway to improve commercial performance and occupancy. The space has been designed so that every seat can see the English Channel's horizon and the Art-Deco style paneling, which is used to create a theatrical effect, with the sea acting as a natural screen.

1 Urban Reef's diverse offerings are knitted together by holistic branding

2 Visual cues are used to impressive effect

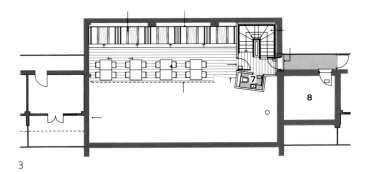

3

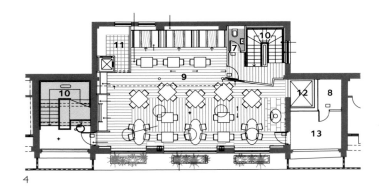

4

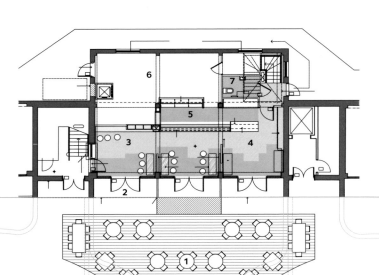

5

6

1 Terrace
2 Entry
3 Café
4 Deli
5 Bar servery
6 Kitchen
7 Restroom
8 Storeroom
9 Restaurant
10 Stairs
11 Food service
12 Elevator
13 Office

7

8

9

3 Mezzanine floor plan

4 First floor plan

5 Ground floor plan

6 1950's furniture, materials, and finishes are used on the first floor

7 Art-Deco style paneling is used to theatrical effect

8 Energetic and snappy colors echo the ground floor's visual theme

9 Urban Reef is a beacon for bar-goers on the UK's south coast

Photography by Darren Ciolli-Leach

THE VIOLET HOUR

CHICAGO, ILLINOIS, USA
Design Bureaux, Inc.

The visual inspiration for the design of The Violet Hour was drawn from the pared-down styles of the early 19th-century English Georgian and French Directoire. The English club and French salon were the precursors of the modern venue for socializing and drinking. This project not only uses stylistic cues from these precedents but more importantly uses spatial references such as the partitioning of space into several smaller rooms, the use of extra high wing-back furniture groupings, and the breaking down of the bar into several separate lengths all to create places of intimacy conducive to the art of conversation. The cocktail takes center stage in each room with the curtained partitions acting to frame the bartenders and the mirrored back bar cabinets highlighting the numerous specialty liquors and ingredients.

The overall look of the bar is seductive with a hint of refinement, comfortable but with moments of luxury. Richer surfaces and colors are contrasted against cleaner more minimal ones, such as the parquet floor and velvet curtains versus the minimalist walls and ceilings. The interior elements have been designed to heighten the sensation of having private experiences within a large active environment.

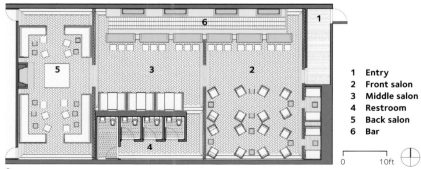

1 Entry
2 Front salon
3 Middle salon
4 Restroom
5 Back salon
6 Bar

0   10ft

1

2

1   The view from the front salon down to the fireplace in the back salon
2   Floor plan
3   One section of the bar
4   Extra high wing-back chairs help to partition space
5   The fireplace in the back salon

Photography by Michael Robinson

3

4

5

THE VOODOO ROOMS

EDINBURGH, UK
Voodoo Rooms Scotland Ltd

1

2

The Voodoo Rooms—comprising a bar, a restaurant, a live music venue, and events rooms—is located in an A-listed Georgian building that was formerly used as a hotel. Spread over two floors, The Voodoo Rooms includes five large rooms with three bars—the main bar, the dining room, The Speakeasy, The Ballroom, and the adjoining American Bar—all of which can operate independently or as a whole for larger events.

Each room has a different feel, but common throughout are the fantastic period ceilings and the black and gold color scheme. The American Bar and dining room are wood paneled and, along with the main bar, are lined with large ornately framed arched windows. The ballroom has a central domed ceiling and twinkling starcloth-clad walls. The Speakeasy is self-contained and located one floor below. This venue specializes in rums, tequilas, and cocktails. The cocktail list was created by manager Shervene Shahbazkhani—a Scottish 42 Below Cocktail World Cup champion—and features an intriguing selection of delicious drinks in four themed sections.

1   Welcome to The Voodoo Rooms
2, 4–6   Main bar
3   The A-listed Georgian building was formerly a hotel

3

4

5

6

Photography by Oscar Munar

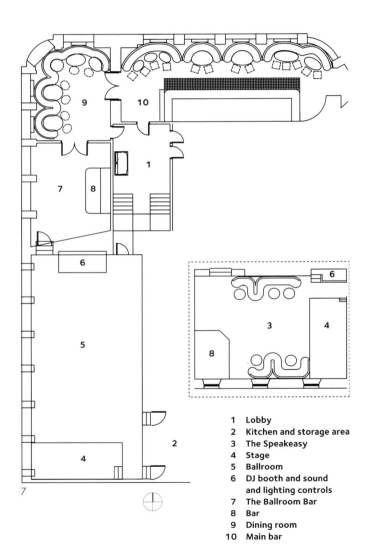

7

1   Lobby
2   Kitchen and storage area
3   The Speakeasy
4   Stage
5   Ballroom
6   DJ booth and sound
    and lighting controls
7   The Ballroom Bar
8   Bar
9   Dining room
10 Main bar

8

9

11

12

13

WHISKEY PARK

ATLANTA, GEORGIA, USA
ICRAVE

1

Whiskey Park, the lounge concept operated by Gerber Group at the W Atlanta Midtown Hotel is a room-by-room narrative of a decadent house, in which touches of Liberace meet contemporary modern hip-hop culture. At the top of the stairs from the lobby, a jeweled portal transports visitors into the Gallery Bar, a double-height room decorated with an oversized angled mirror and dramatic pink light boxes. In the Crystal Lounge, gold mirrors, bold graphics, and Fendi-inspired furniture create a flashy and elaborately styled environment.

Moving from room to room, patrons eventually encounter the Vault Room, a secret back area designed for the ultra VIP. Faceted custom-cut MDF panels are embedded with pinpoint crystal LED lights, giving visitors the sense that they have entered a secret vault filled with jewels and precious possessions. This private, intimate space features dark-wood flooring, black-lacquered walls, and a bar set among red-and-black mosaic tiles.

1   Dramatic, oversized pink light boxes give off a sexy glow
    in the Gallery Bar

2   Entrance to the Vault Room

1 Entry
2 Main bar
3 Gallery bar
4 Elevator
5 Open to below
6 Service bar
7 Vault Room
8 Back of house
9 Men's restroom
10 Women's restroom
11 Storage
12 Chase
13 Electrical room
14 Outdoor lounge
15 Crystal Lounge

3

4

5

6

7

8

Photography by John Bartelstone

iNDEX OF ARCHITECTS & DESIGNERS